D1306855

CRYSTALS

to *empower* you

CRYSTALS

to *empower* you

JUDY HALL

**Use crystals and the Law of Attraction
to manifest abundance, wellbeing
and happiness**

WALKING
STICK
PRESS

Published in the U.S. by Walking Stick Press, an imprint of F+W Media, Inc.
10151 Carver Road, Suite #200, Blue Ash, OH 45242
(800) 289-0963

First published in Great Britain in 2013 by
Godsfield Press, a division of Octopus Publishing Group Ltd
Endeavour House
189 Shaftesbury Avenue
London
WC2H 8JY
www.octopusbooks.co.uk

Copyright © Octopus Publishing Group Ltd 2013
Text copyright © Judy Hall 2013

All rights reserved. No part of this work may be reproduced or utilized in
any form or by any means, electronic or mechanical, including photocopying,
recording or by any information storage and retrieval system, without the
prior written permission of the publisher.

Judy Hall asserts the moral right to be identified as the author of this work.

ISBN 978-1-59963-718-1

A CIP catalogue record for this book is available from the British Library.

Printed and bound in China.

10 9 8 7 6 5 4 3 2

DISCLAIMER

No medical claims are made for the stones in this book, and the information given is not
intended to act as a substitute for medical treatment. The healing properties are given for
guidance only and are, for the most part, based on anecdotal evidence and/or traditional
therapeutic use. If in any doubt about their use, consult a crystal-healing practitioner. In the
context of this book, illness is a dis-ease, the final manifestation of spiritual, environmental,
psychological, karmic, emotional or mental imbalance or distress. Healing means bringing
mind, body and spirit back into balance and facilitating evolution for the soul; it does not
imply a cure. In accordance with crystal-healing consensus, all stones are referred to as
crystals, regardless of whether or not they have a crystalline structure.

CONTENTS

PART ONE

Manifesting techniques 18

Introduction

Manifesting with crystals is really easy: they are amazing tools. You don't need any special skills or pre-knowledge; you simply need to be willing to spend a few moments getting to know your crystals and following the easy, step-by-step instructions that accompany each crystal profile.

MANIFESTING AND THE LAW OF ATTRACTION

However, manifesting is not something you do – it is what you are. Manifesting is an outward expression of your inner being. It makes visible your background thoughts and feelings and expresses your core self. We all manifest every second of every day. With each thought, emotion and belief that passes through us, we create our reality, whether or not we intend to. The secret is to bring the process consciously under your direction. When Socrates said that the unexamined life was not worth living – in his insistence that each belief should be questioned, each area of doubt probed, each smidgen of unknowing examined – he stated a profound truth. If we do not examine our inner life, and those thoughts, feelings and beliefs that underlie what we experience externally, how can we possibly expect to influence our outer life?

How can we manifest what we seek if we haven't examined very carefully a limiting belief and its wider implications, and if we haven't looked at the mental filters through which we view the world? The Law of Attraction says that we draw back to us what we give out ('like attracts like'); that each thought we have, each emotion, each core belief creates what we experience from moment to moment. How can we manifest what we most desire if, deep down, we don't believe we deserve it? How can we fulfil our true potential if we are following someone else's expectations of us? And – perhaps the deepest question of all – how can we successfully manifest something that goes against our soul-plan?

These are fundamental questions that we will address as we journey together through this book. We'll explore the process of manifestation in all its wonderment and delight – as well as the pitfalls on the path. We'll also examine why it may be more beneficial for us not to manifest what we think we need; or to manifest what seems to be the very opposite of what we thought we wanted. And we'll learn how to create our own magical reality through directed thought.

We'll be using the perfect tools to assist us in the manifestation process: crystals and some simple rituals and layouts. Crystals have been around since the dawn of prehistory; they were always regarded as sacred, therapeutic and, above all, magical. Holding a magnetic charge, crystals interceded with the gods to create good fortune, offer protection and good luck, and bring about wellbeing on all levels. They still assist us in doing this today – when we move beyond the limitations of what we expect and tap into their (and our own) true magical potential.

THE PRINCIPLES OF MANIFESTING

Manifesting is the result of thoughts and feelings projected out to the world. The more conscious the intention and the more directed the thought, the more positive the result is. Thoughts and feelings are vibrations that attract – or repel – whatever you wish to manifest. The secret of successful manifesting is to realize that every thought (and feeling) is a request that is picked up by the universe, magnified and sent back.

What is manifesting?

Manifesting is an ongoing process of creation that shapes the fundamental energy of the universe. It is not something you do once, then sit back and wait for the outcome. It is a process that may be conscious or unconscious, benevolent or derailing. The saying 'what goes around, comes around' embodies a deep truth. Your thoughts and wishes are instructions that are picked up, magnified and returned to you: dispassionately, but accurately and in abundance. So the more conscious you are – the more focused, positive and aware you are of all that goes on within your head – and the more contented your heart, the more positively you will manifest. The more you choose to have good feelings and constructive thoughts, the more your world mirrors them back to you. The better choices you make, the more you can achieve. True creation actually starts in the heart rather than the head. If there are contradictions within you – if the part that is unconscious is putting out one message while your conscious mind is putting out another – then confusion and negative manifestation will result. Feeling blessed allows you to be blest. So count your blessings each day!

Some people seem to believe that it is the universe's task to give them what they want – to respond to petitions for 'more money', 'more love', 'a better life'. They look to something 'out there' to create on their behalf. But that is akin to scientists who are studying consciousness asking how matter (the brain) creates the mind. They would be much better off asking how mind (consciousness) shapes matter into the material world and all that manifests. Other people look at the world through a filter of lack – feeling hard done by and undeserving – and want someone to make it all better for them.

Those who make such demands are living their lives backward. They think that if they have more of what they so desperately desire, they will be happier. In truth, the more contented they are inside, and the more they like who they are and express that to the world, the more that joy radiates out and attracts back to them an abundant life. It creates a self-fulfilling prophecy, a benevolent gifting circle. And they may well find that they don't actually need more money (or whatever they were demanding), as that was merely to fill an inner vacuum caused by lack of connection with their core self in all its amazing wonder-fullness.

'Asking the universe' gives away your own power to create. It puts the power to direct your life firmly in the hands of A.N. Other – whether that is God, the universe, the cosmos, or whatever. Take back that power (see Malachite, pages 44–47), and you become the creator of your own world. We'll be looking at personal manifestation, co-creation and soul-creation later on.

Am I asking for the right thing?

So, you've tried the manifestation process and it hasn't worked? You've put in your cosmic order, tried to uncover 'The Secret', followed the Law of Attraction and, as far as you can see, your deepest desire hasn't yet manifested. Or has it, and you simply haven't realized what that deepest desire actually was? Continual blocking may be a sign that there is something fundamentally confused or unwise about what you seek. It may be that there are core beliefs, karmic debts or soul-intentions

that are not in accord with manifesting what you truly need (see Malachite, pages 44–47). You may be asking for something that is inauspicious for your soul-growth (see Trigonic Quartz, pages 146–49).

Ineffective manifestation can also be a sign that you are not putting out your request and then letting it go. Constant worrying will block the process, as will a deep emotional investment in the outcome, or following someone else's dream. As the Mexican actress Salma Hayek pointed out: 'If you enjoy the process, it's your dream. If you are enduring the process, just desperate for the result, it's somebody else's dream.' So, when formulating your intention, ensure it is what *you* truly desire for yourself.

Am I asking in the right way?

As I was reminded just the other day, you must be precise in what you ask for, paying attention to the way you phrase it, to avoid 'unthinking'

manifesting. Some time ago I bought a block of premium bonds. It was an exciting prospect, with numbers randomly chosen generating monthly prizes, both large and small. How serendipitous was that? Each month I had the pleasure of opening an envelope that might surprise me with a big win. In the first year the return was well above what I would have received had I invested the money safely. Later I reinvested it. Then I didn't receive any cheques for several months. When I did, it was for the minimum amount. My thought on opening it was: 'Thank you, but I wanted more.' The next month there were five cheques: each for the minimum amount. I literally got back what I had asked for: more of the same. What I should have said was: 'Thank you, but next month I want a large amount.' A valuable lesson, which reminded me to catch every thought I have and ensure it is formulated appropriately.

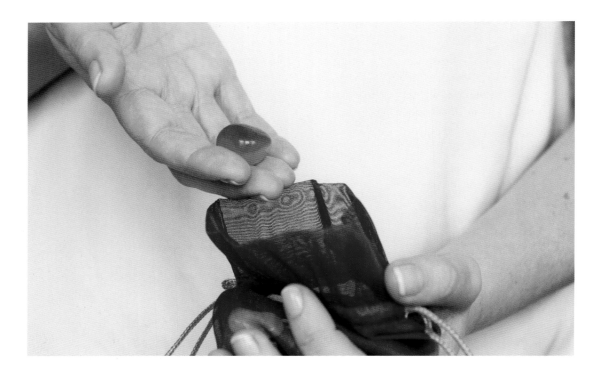

How do I work with manifestation?

Each of the spreads in Part Two of this book (pages 34–155) introduces a way of manifesting for a specific purpose, crystals to assist, and easy-to-follow activations to help you put the manifesting into practice. Each can be adapted and applied to other purposes. You don't need to spend a lot of time on this; nothing in the book takes longer than half an hour, and many of the activations take far less time. All you need to do is ensure that your heart and head, your conscious, subconscious and unconscious minds and your intention are congruent (in harmony) and aligned to your true purpose – and you know precisely what that is.

What skills do I need to cultivate?

Powerful feelings (not emotions, which have judgments attached) are key. True creation starts in the heart rather than the head. The secret is to feel deeply what you seek, picture what it is like when it manifests, step into it and then let go. Trust the process. Throughout this book you'll learn how to focus your intention, maintain total presence and hold your centre. You'll also learn how to go with the flow and allow. When manifesting, it is counterproductive to force anything; it's all about opening your inner being. You'll learn to put aside your ego and let the highest part of yourself manifest what is best for you and those around you.

Key skills

- FOCUSED INTENTION: keep your mind and feelings focused on a positive outcome now

- TOTAL PRESENCE: stay fully in the present moment, and don't hark back to the past or project yourself forward into the future

- INTROSPECTION AND CONTEMPLATION: catch those thoughts and feelings that would otherwise trip you up

- **HOLDING YOUR CENTRE**: stay in your core self, with congruent beliefs
- **CHOOSING TO HAVE GOOD FEELINGS AND CONSTRUCTIVE THOUGHTS**: step out of negative, self-limiting feelings into a positive, radiant sense of wellbeing, joy and inner enrichment
- **NON-JUDGMENT**: avoid judgment on whether things are 'good' or 'bad'
- **BEING AND ALLOWING**: stay in the manifesting flow of who you are at your core
- **SETTING GOALS AND MAKING CHOICES**: break down into achievable steps whatever you seek
- **TRUST**: expect that the process will have a good outcome
- **GRATITUDE**: thank yourself and the universe for what is manifested
- **FLOW, OPENNESS TO CHANGE**: allow yourself to be surprised by serendipity (making fortunate discoveries by accident) and the unexpected
- **ACCEPTANCE**: receive with grace and gratitude any gifts that you receive, whatever the source may be

RIGHT TIMING

Part of the skill of manifesting is learning not to push against the river, but rather to use the force of the river to turn things your way. This is an ongoing process – an instant result is not necessarily how manifesting works. It is about allowing, not doing; about being open to, rather than insisting. If there is a delay, when you look back you'll see that the timing was perfect.

Following soul-timing

There is a part of you that has a much wider perspective than the small 'you' living here on the Earth. I call this the soul. It is an eternal being with a very long life-history – some of which is lived on Earth and some in other dimensions. We are used to thinking of ourselves as all of a piece: one indivisible being that is here, now. But experience says there is a much more expanded you, which holds the secret of right timing, as it has access to your soul-plan. It knows what is to come, and can call upon skills and abilities developed in other lifetimes to assist you. As the musician Ray Charles put it, a soul is like electricity – we don't really know what it is, but its force can light up a room. Cooperating with this expanded self dynamically accelerates the manifestation process, as does trusting that the manifestation comes at exactly the right moment for you.

Seasons and cycles

When William Shakespeare wrote, 'There is a tide in the affairs of men, which, taken at the flood, leads on to fortune; omitted, all the voyage of their life is bound in shallows and in miseries', he was talking not only about taking advantage of opportunities that arise, but also about right timing. As an astrologer, I follow the seasons and cycles of the zodiac to assist my manifesting. I plant my seed at the dark of the moon so that it develops and comes to fruition at full moon. My rituals are carried out at those times. The dates of the new and full moons are easily accessible and represent potent timing. The same applies to the cycle of the year. My mentor, Christine Hartley, advised me never to start a project in the weeks immediately before the Winter Solstice on 21 December because, in the northern hemisphere, these were traditionally fallow days when things should be allowed to die, before starting anew (in the southern hemisphere this would be the Summer Solstice on 21 June). Much more sensible, she said, to begin at the first new moon after the solstice.

The greater cycle of Jupiter and the sun set bigger plans in motion, because they signal a whole new 12-year cycle of opportunity that occurs roughly at the ages of 12, 24, 36, and so on. But you don't have to wait for these 'trigger' birthdays to begin – simply ensure that the process of allowing, rather than forcing, guides your timing.

A sense of lack

Perhaps the biggest pitfall is to come from a place of 'lack': feeling that something is missing that you have to fill. There is an inner aching emptiness that (or so you believe) money, food, a lover or a change of environment will fill. However, if what you have inside is lack, then what will manifest is more of the same. Lack begets lack, emptiness begets emptiness. So to manifest successfully you need to come from a place of inner contentment.

Learning to receive

Not being open to receiving is a powerful block on manifesting. If you can't receive from other people and are unable to show gratitude for the gifts they – or the universe – are willing to share with you, you cannot expect the universe to support your manifesting. If you don't feel gratitude for the small things, the universe is unlikely to shower you with abundance.

Non-acceptance blocks the flow. For instance, Claire spent enormous amounts of money on presents for other people and yet hated receiving gifts herself. When she was on the receiving end she would rant and rage because the giver, in her view, couldn't afford the present they had so thoughtfully chosen for her. She took away all the joy of giving to her, but was surprised when she couldn't manifest a lottery win. If she had been able to receive joyfully, that would have opened the flow of abundance for her. Check out whether you are open to receive.

WHAT TRIPS YOU UP?

If, despite your best efforts, your manifesting isn't working, it's time to examine what is tripping you up. You may be caught in a cycle of non-expectation, arising from experiences that constantly 'proved' your deepest fears – or so it seems. Or you may be asking for things that are unrealistic or inappropriate, too specific or too nebulous. Or you may be too attached to the outcome. Identifying these hidden pitfalls enables you to replace them with positive expectations.

Core expectations and background beliefs

What you expect to happen happens. It arises from limiting core beliefs held at a deep, unconscious level. Such beliefs may be based on karmic expectations (what we have come to believe will happen, based on past experience) from other lives, childhood experience or toxic ancestral patterns that create self-fulfilling prophecies. If you've been told that you need to live within your limitations, accept restrictions and expect problems, then that is the life you will manifest. Successful manifesting requires that negative background thoughts and limiting beliefs are transformed.

As a friend of mine put it: 'To consider that every thought that rattled around in my brain was really an instruction made me determined to unbury all those useless beliefs that are bad instructions to the universe.' She had realized that: 'The thing with beliefs is that they cannot be evaluated as true or false, based on our life experience. We get caught in this cycle: I have this belief, which instructs the universe to give me things that make this belief true, so now I have proof that my belief is true. So it becomes necessary to evaluate our belief system not on what is "true", but on whether that belief is useful or not, and what kind of instruction it is really giving to the universe.'

I couldn't agree more, and as you work through this book you will uncover those hidden instructions.

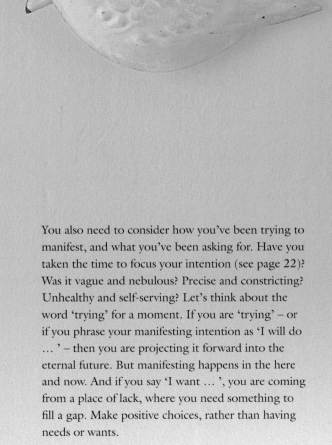

You also need to consider how you've been trying to manifest, and what you've been asking for. Have you taken the time to focus your intention (see page 22)? Was it vague and nebulous? Precise and constricting? Unhealthy and self-serving? Let's think about the word 'trying' for a moment. If you are 'trying' – or if you phrase your manifesting intention as 'I will do …' – then you are projecting it forward into the eternal future. But manifesting happens in the here and now. And if you say 'I want … ', you are coming from a place of lack, where you need something to fill a gap. Make positive choices, rather than having needs or wants.

PROBLEMS AND ANTIDOTES

- PROBLEM: **Do you believe 'It's been that way, so it will always be that way?'**
  ANTIDOTE: 'I am the author of my own destiny, I create my world.'

- PROBLEM: **Are many of your beliefs false and do they no longer serve you?**
  ANTIDOTE: the Rutilated Quartz placement on page 52.

- PROBLEM: **Do you have thoughts and expectations that were implanted by someone else?**
  ANTIDOTE: the Malachite meditation on page 46 and the Rutilated Quartz placement on page 52.

- PROBLEM: **Do you have vague aspirations or needs, rather than setting achievable goals?**
  ANTIDOTE: break your manifesting down into small pieces, but allow for serendipity too (see Setting an intention, page 22).

- PROBLEM: **Do you expect to grow through struggle?**
  ANTIDOTE: 'I grow through joy and expanded awareness' (see Aurora Quartz, pages 134–37).

- PROBLEM: **Have you ever said: 'I can't help it, it's my karma.'**
  ANTIDOTE: renegotiate your soul-contracts and release yourself (see Wind Fossil Agate, pages 56–59).

- PROBLEM: **Do you often find yourself thinking, 'I don't deserve this?'**
  ANTIDOTE: change the programme! 'I deserve every good thing, happiness, wellbeing, riches and fulfilment' (see Citrine, pages 62–65).

- PROBLEM: **Are your instructions to the universe centred around what you don't want, rather than what you seek to manifest?**
  ANTIDOTE: phrase your manifesting intentions in the positive, present tense.

- PROBLEM: **Have you ever told yourself that there are no victims, only volunteers?**
  ANTIDOTE: remind yourself that spiritual growth can be joyful, easy and playful.

- PROBLEM: **Are you overly attached to the outcome, or do you worry about it continually?**
  ANTIDOTE: step out of your own way. Do the manifesting process and then let go – trust the process.

- PROBLEM: **Are you unable to receive gifts from others?**
  ANTIDOTE: accept every gift, no matter how large or small, with a huge smile and a heartfelt 'Thank you'.

- PROBLEM: **Do you feel powerless and helpless, trapped in a cycle of poverty and lack?**
  ANTIDOTE: Reclaim your power (see Malachite pages 44–47) and create abundance (see Citrine, pages 62–65).

Do you truly believe you can shift the level at which you manifest? *Do it now!*

Breaking the circle

The vicious circle of toxic expectation can be broken by the activations that follow and by a sense of joyful expectation. The activations are very easy – many of them take only a few minutes, some just a little longer. But you must actually put in the work, not just think about it.

You can start by asking yourself simple questions and listening to the answers that pop into your mind before you have a chance to censor them. Once you've caught hold of these background thoughts, you can transform them. Get into the habit of monitoring every stray thought that passes through your mind and asking yourself, 'Is that useful?'; if not, let it go. Similarly you need to catch the depressive feelings that prevent you from experiencing joy.

HOW TO USE THIS BOOK

Manifesting with crystals is so simple. Each crystal profile (see Part Two) introduces a core process of manifestation and demonstrates how to harness the power of the crystal, while at the same time encouraging you to take responsibility for the outcome. Rather than saying 'Do it this way', the profile helps you sense the energy of crystals, choose the appropriate one and work with it in an interactive process, to generate inner security and a real sense of wellbeing.

Personalizing your manifesting

Everything in this book has been designed to be quick and easy, and to create a smooth flow of manifesting. Part One introduces the basic techniques and helps you develop the skills that facilitate manifesting. In Part Two you'll explore abundance and what can enrich your life, in addition to money. You'll carry out visualizations, rituals and layouts with crystals that appeal to you. This personalizes and powerfully enhances the manifestation process. The activations for each crystal can be expanded and the skills transferred to working with other crystal tools.

So, where do I start?

This book has been carefully planned in an order that helps you uncover anything that may be tripping you up, and then expands your manifesting skills. So once you've familiarized yourself with the basic techniques in Part One (see pages 18–33), stepping into your power (see page 42), de-cluttering your mind (see page 48) and creating abundance (see page 60) represent a great way to begin. It may also be beneficial to take a look at clearing your karma (see page 54).

Once you've made a decision as to which approach to take, cleanse and activate your crystals (see pages 24–25 and 33) and get started. Remember to set aside sufficient time in a quiet space.

You may have bought the book with a specific purpose in mind. If so, once you've read Part One, you can identify in Part Two (see pages 34–155) the process that most closely matches your intention. Say you wish to find the right job – one with better pay and prospects, but one that is also fulfilling. You can take several approaches to this. You could simply adapt the Jade attraction layout (page 88) to draw the job to you. But if you seek courage to apply for the job in the first place, Carnelian (pages 92–95) would assist you, as would Garnet (pages 104–107), Malachite (page 44–47), Wind Fossil Agate (pages 56–59) or Goldstone (pages 68–71). You could also try the visualization to attract a mentor (page 124). Or you could check out your soul-plan with Trigonic Quartz (pages 146–49). Each approach comes from a slightly different angle, and you could of course work with them all to identify exactly what kind of job would be most fulfilling, what would be the most appropriate way of tackling it and how to manifest it. This is where taking responsibility comes in – as does serendipity.

Manifesting techniques

Everything needs a structure through which to manifest, especially the subtle energies of thought and intention. With their crystalline matrix, crystals absorb, hold and radiate energy and, perhaps more importantly, have been used as part of the manifesting process for thousands of years. By virtue of long use, therefore, they are already imbued with the power of belief and carry a manifesting programme within them that just needs activating.

Each crystal has its own unique power, which can be harnessed to manifest your deepest desires. Our world is made up of consciousness: energy and matter. Light, sound and vibration underpin creation. Everything resonates at different frequencies, and crystals can bridge those frequencies, bringing your consciousness into harmony with whatever you seek.

HOW TO MEET YOUR MAGICAL SELF

Before we go any further, it's time for you to know that you are a magical being; to recognize that you create your world in every moment – the very essence of magic. What you see or do, what you react or respond to, what you think or feel is powerful beyond measure. It brings your world into being. Inside you is a magical self waiting to be released, which manifests what you desire easily and effortlessly.

THE MAGICAL SELF

Our magical self can transcend time and space, moving effortlessly beyond our three-dimensional world, seeing past its illusions and delusions, into a place where everything is possible and our potential is unlimited.

If you get into the habit of noticing all the small ways in which your manifestation works, you will soon come to recognize the amazing magical potency of your true self. To continue the cycle of magical manifestation, show gratitude and feel blessed.

ACTIVATING YOUR MAGICAL SELF

- Tell yourself every morning as you awake, 'I am a magical being. I manifest whatever I most desire. I am powerful, purposeful and wise.' Believe it!

- Focus your intention, and your attention, on all things positive.

- Trust yourself and your intuition for a whole day. Note down all your successes, then build on them each day that follows.

- If you had any doubts, erase them and replace them with 'can do'. Find the positive opposite to any negative thought or belief about yourself, and state it out loud in the present tense: 'I am … '

- Recognize that there are no limits to who you are.

- Change your perception of yourself and your world – suspend your judgment.

- Do the impossible.

- Take an inventory of all the habits and thoughts you have that are no longer relevant to the present moment. Delete it and replace it with your own personal empowerment activation.

- Capitalize on the power of your imagination. In your mind's eye create a picture of exactly how you'd like to be and what you'd do in a perfect world. Once it's built up strongly in your mind and you can feel how it is to be that way, wave a magic crystal wand to bring it into being in the everyday.

- Meditate with your magical self crystal each day to strengthen your connection to your magical self and carry your crystal with you each day.

MEETING YOUR MAGICAL SELF MEDITATION

You can use any crystal you like for this activation. Manifestation Quartz (pages 38–41), Brandenberg (pages 140–43) or Merlinite (pages 152–55) is particularly suitable.

1 Hold your crystal in your hands and feel its energy radiating out into the manifestation chakras (energy linkage points between the physical and subtle bodies, see page 30) in your palms.

2 Feel how this energy activates your magical self – the part of you that can see so much further than the everyday self; the part that is all-powerful, wise and all-knowing; the part that can move through time and space.

3 Expand into this magical self, welcoming and embracing it. This is the you that you truly are. Now send that magical self out to the universe.

FOCUSED INTENTION

Focused intention is thought that is purposefully directed toward whatever you seek to manifest. Holding an intention is different from willing something into being. Intention is a 'delighted expectancy' that you feel, with all the power of your being, and then let go of. Maintaining mental and emotional detachment from the outcome assists in manifesting intention. Without clarity of intention, your manifesting cannot function.

REFINING YOUR INTENTION

Intention is a highly ordered, subtle energy that is capable of transforming the physical world. To do this you need to have clarity of intention. Intention without contradiction, hidden agendas, conflict or ambiguity is one of the most powerful forces in

the universe. Holding a positive intention and knowing when to let it go is one of the great secrets of manifesting. Being emotionally invested is counterproductive, but being fully involved – letting your body and mind feel what it's like when whatever you seek manifests – puts your intention into being.

Before you state your intention, you need to clarify it. Keep asking yourself, 'What is it that I really seek?' 'Is it this, or something else?' 'Is this based on need and a sense of lack?' 'What would enrich me?' Refine this until you get to the core. If you find that you are working from negative aspirations, turn them around into positive goals. Instead of focusing on a need for more money, for example, you could use the positive affirmation (or saying): 'Prosperity flows to me, and through me, right now. My intention is that all my needs are met with ease and grace. Thank you.'

SETTING AN INTENTION

Once you have found the core of whatever you wish to manifest, ask for that which you seek. Phrase your intention in as short and pithy a sentence as possible – and in the present tense. State it out loud, let yourself feel how it is when it manifests, and then let it go, sending it out to the universe, trusting that it will return fulfilled.

Support your manifesting with the crystals and rituals described in this book, and remember to show gratitude for all the ways (big or small) in which your intention is fulfilled.

DREAMING WISHES INTO REALITY

Quartz is the perfect crystal to support your dreams and turn them into reality. This crystal is available in many shapes and forms. It absorbs, generates, amplifies and releases energy as appropriate, and is excellent for holding a manifestation activation. If Quartz is struck in the dark it generates a visible spark of light, so it was always considered a magical stone. Ancient stonebooks (which described the magical and healing properties of stones) are filled with stories of its miraculous powers – and how it formed from frozen ice, which, when compressed, transformed into the sparkling crystal. As you will see,

manifesting with Quartz is a really easy process. Always ensure that you use a cleansed activated crystal (see pages 33–34).

USING QUARTZ TO AMPLIFY YOUR WISHES

1 Hold your Quartz in your hands and ask that it works with you for your highest good.

2 Picture whatever your dream is, as clearly and intensely as possible. Feel all the joy of having that dream come true. Let yourself really feel the power of the dream and how it is when you manifest it in your life. Let that power flow into the crystal in your hand, and ask the crystal to manifest the dream.

3 Put the crystal where you will see it often, or keep it in your pocket to remind you of your dream.

MANIFESTING WITH YOUR CRYSTALS

Choosing and manifesting with crystals is easy, once you identify the correct stone for your purpose. Read the section relating to what you wish to manifest (see Part Two, pages 36–155), check out the tools that are available to you (see below), then look at the crystals illustrated in this book and see which ones speak to you or which you already have in your collection. Finally, use your crystals to manifest your desire.

CHOOSING YOUR CRYSTALS

When you have identified appropriate stones, visit a crystal store in person or online, if you do not already have the crystals to hand. Remember that biggest is not necessarily best, nor is the most beautiful crystal the most powerful one. Non-gem-quality stones have the same attributes as the more expensive faceted forms with their shaped, polished sides. Tumbled (polished) stones are robust and ideal for layouts, or pattern grids. If you are using faceted gemstones, these are best set as jewellery, to protect them.

Handling stones enables 'your' crystal to be attracted to you. Most crystal stores offer a wide choice. If you plunge your hand into a tub of crystals, the right one will stick to your fingers. If a particular crystal catches your eye as you enter the store, this is the one for you.

DEDICATING AND ACTIVATING YOUR CRYSTALS

Before a crystal works with you it needs to be dedicated to your highest good and activated to manifest your wishes. Dedicating it 'to your highest good' means that the crystal cannot be used in a way that harms others, even inadvertently; at the

highest level we are all connected and, as crystals remind us, we are one.

Paradoxically, you need to activate a crystal with focused intention (see page 22) and yet not limit it by being too specific. 'This or something better' opens the way for serendipity to come into your life. To activate the crystal, simply hold it between your hands and say out loud, 'I dedicate this crystal to my highest good and that of others. I ask that it assist me with manifesting . . . [name your wish]. This or something better.' Remember that crystals are living beings, so always treat them with respect.

ATTUNING TO YOUR CRYSTAL

Your crystal and your own manifestation powers work together in synergy (cooperation). To connect to the full power of your crystal, hold it in your hands and feel its power radiating into the manifestation chakras (see page 30) on your palms, then out into your whole being.

DEPROGRAMMING YOUR CRYSTAL

When your crystal has fulfilled its present purpose (or if it has come to you with a program already installed), hold it in your hands and thank it for its work, but state clearly that the purpose is no longer needed, so it can be dissolved, along with anything programmed in by anyone else. Cleanse the crystal thoroughly with spring water, or by placing it in brown rice overnight. Then re-energize it in the sun, wrap it up and place it in a drawer until it is needed.

CRYSTAL SHAPES

Part of the magic of crystal manifesting lies in the crystals' subtle geometric form. Crystals may be raw, faceted, polished, tumbled or pointed.

Tumbled or polished stones work well for layouts and for carrying in your pocket; they are comfortable to place on your body. Raw stones can also be used in layouts. Faceted stones are more appropriate for jewellery. Stones that have been polished or shaped into spheres or pleasing tactile shapes are great for holding in your hands. But the underlying energetic crystalline structure remains the same, whatever form the outer manifestation takes.

Crystals with points draw energy down or push it away, depending on which direction they face. With the point facing down toward you or inward, they draw cosmic energy down into a layout or into your body. With the point facing outward or away from you, they draw off negative energy for transmutation – a change for the better in energy. If you are laying out a cleansing grid, for instance, you could place one stone at your feet pointing away from you, to draw off negativity, and one above your head pointing toward your crown, to draw light in. This means that no 'spaces' are left in your energy field. A vacuum where you have let go of toxicity soon refills with more of the same, if you don't consciously refill it with positive energy.

Remember to cleanse your crystals regularly (see page 33), particularly those that you wear and those that you use to draw off negative beliefs or implanted thoughts.

YOUR MANIFESTING TOOLS

Throughout this book you will use a variety of methods to connect to your crystal's power and manifest your intention, including focused visualizations, guided meditations, layouts, grids and rituals.

VISUALIZATION AND GUIDED MEDITATION

The visualizations in this book are pictures that you can see in your mind's eye. Looking up to the space above and between your eyebrows, while keeping your eyes closed, stimulates images to form on an inner 'screen'. If the images don't form, project the screen (still with your eyes shut) a little way in front of you: take your attention to that point between the eyebrows and then let it move forward. With a little practice you will soon get the hang of this. Trying to force images is counterproductive, so be patient and aware that

there are many ways of 'seeing' and sensing, some of which do not involve pictures or words, but rather an inner knowing.

Many people are kinesthetic – that is, they *feel* things rather than see them. So if you don't 'see', simply act. You just need to be able to feel yourself moving out of everyday consciousness and into inner space, and this is facilitated by the energy of the crystals. The beauty of using crystals is that the energy of the stone conveys you through the journey and stimulates insights for you. When you ask questions, be prepared for the answers to arrive as though you are hearing an inner voice or they are arising spontaneously in your mind (see Malachite meditation, page 46); or they may come through something that you hear in the external world. You may find it easier to follow the visualizations and guided meditations in this book if you record them first, with appropriate pauses.

LAYOUTS AND GRIDS

Using grids is the art of placing crystals around a person or place for energy enhancement, attraction, release or protection. Although a grid is laid out flat, it creates a multi-dimensional energy web around it. Each layout, or pattern, has a specific purpose and effect; many different crystals can be used, and the layouts can be adapted to different purposes. You need to connect to the power of your crystal and open your manifestation chakras (see page 30) before laying the stones out. Always lay the crystals down slowly, with focused intention and due ceremony.

Use the power of your mind or a wand to join grids. Allow universal energy to flow in through your crown chakra (top of your head), down the arm to the hand holding the wand, into the manifestation chakra (palm) and into the wand. Do not use your own energy.

TRIANGLE: Triangulation neutralizes negative energy and brings in positive energy. It also creates a safe space and magnetizes it for maximum attraction of beneficial energies. Place one crystal centrally and two others opposite and below, with the angles equal, if possible. Connect the points with a wand to strengthen the grid.

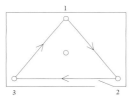

SPIRAL: Spirals are the dance of life made manifest. A universal symbol of energy, a clockwise spiral [A] draws energy in, while a counter-clockwise spiral [B] releases it out to the universe. If you need to release something to make way for a new situation, draw a counter-clockwise spiral. Letting go creates a space into which something new can manifest. You can also use a counter-clockwise spiral to send good things out to the universe to benefit others, so that they ultimately return amplified one-thousandfold by your generosity. If you need to draw cosmic assistance to you, draw a clockwise spiral.

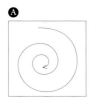

FIVE-POINTED STAR: This is a useful protection layout or caller-in of love, abundance and healing. It is the traditional shape for grounding your wishes. Standing or lying in the star enhances your energy and attraction factor. Follow the direction of the arrows on the diagram when placing the crystals, and remember to connect to the starting crystal to complete the circuit.

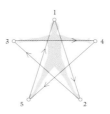
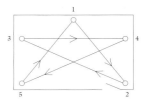

STAR OF DAVID: This is a traditional protection layout that represents the union of masculine and feminine, and perfect balance. A symbol for the heart, it creates the perfect manifestation space for something new to emerge. Lay the first triangle (point up to release energy, point down to draw it in) and join up the points with a wand. Now lay another triangle on top, the other way up, and join up the points. It is also possible to draw a continuous six-pointed star that creates an active energy net [A]; and to lay two six-pointed stars on top of each other (with the top one slightly rotated) to form a 12-pointed star of manifestation [B].

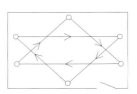

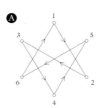
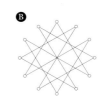

RITUALS

Rituals harness the power of your mind and honour your intentions. Traditionally celebrants performed rituals within a purified, sacred space. You can 'smudge' the space (use the smoke from sage, sweetgrass or other herbs to purify its energies) or spray it with a proprietary space-cleanser. You can wear a robe, but this isn't necessary; it does make the ritual feel special if you bathe beforehand and put on clean clothes, but it is more important that you carry it out with your attention and your emotions fully engaged in the process. Ensure that you are not disturbed during the ritual. Music can assist, as can candles and incense, but it is your joyful intention and focus that bring success.

ALTARS

When you set up an altar, you are creating a sacred space – somewhere to honour your intentions and All That Is. Altars need to be situated where they will not be disturbed (see Manifestation Quartz activation, page 40). You can place on your altar special objects, crystals, candles (see below), photographs and so on. If you place photographs of the things you wish to manifest, this does not mean you are worshipping the object: you are simply using the altar as a focus for your manifesting. Always keep your altar clean and tidy, with fresh flowers and candles as appropriate. It will benefit from a daily smudging or spray with a crystal cleanser.

CANDLES

A candle traditionally symbolizes transmutation and your inner light. Coloured candles support the manifesting process. Light whichever colour is appropriate for your rituals and your altar:

COLOUR	EFFECTS
White	Radiates purity and tranquillity.
Pink	Invokes love.
Red	Resolves conflicts.
Orange	Ensures success.
Green	Creates prosperity
Yellow	Facilitates successful studies and journeys.
Blue	Attracts healing.
Indigo	Releases limitations.
Lilac	Stimulates spirituality and psychic gifts.

EMBODYING YOUR DESIRES

Although your mind plays an important part in conceiving what you wish to manifest, research has shown that your physical body and the stance you adopt profoundly affect the outcome. You can stimulate successful manifesting with some easy body-posturing. A confident stance always enhances the manifestation process, as does being relaxed and at ease rather than tense and intense.

Kinesthesia, or body-sensing, also plays an important role in intuition, so pay attention to your gut feelings whenever you formulate an intention or a desire to manifest.

To support your intention and activate willpower

This is particularly helpful when you seek to change a pattern of behaviour before you manifest something new, or to hold an intention in the face of someone else's opposition or doubt.

- If you have to say no: fold your arms over your solar plexus (just above your navel) while holding your crystal. This also works when you feel in need of support.
- Tense your muscles as you speak your intention, or walk backward. Strange though it sounds, this strengthens your intention.

To put out a request

When stating your intention or making a request, extend your left arm to its full extent, holding your manifesting crystal as you do so. Bend your right arm at the elbow. Bring your hand up to your forehead over your third eye (in the centre of your forehead, between and slightly above your eyebrows). Hold that pose for a few moments as your desires wing their way into physical manifestation. Or it may feel more natural to reverse your hands (especially if you are left-handed), extending your right hand; do whatever feels right for you.

To think creatively

You can make your thoughts more creative, or change a deeply embedded response, using simple eye movements.

- To stimulate your creativity, hold your crystal as far to the left as possible; follow it with your eyes, but without moving your head, as you move it to the right. Repeat six times.
- To change an ingrained thought pattern, move your crystal to the left, then down, then across to the bottom right, then up to the top right and back to the left, following it with your eyes. Repeat three times. (You may need to change direction, depending on which is your dominant eye. To test dominance of hand or eye, close your eyes and touch your nose with each hand in turn. Whichever hand touches the centre of your nose is dominant.)

YOUR MANIFESTATION CHAKRAS

Manifestation chakras are what we use to sense crystal energies, but these chakras – or energy linkage points – are also part of the manifestation process. They are receptive (receiving energy) and expressive (radiating it). So they are intimately connected to your ability to receive and to generate. They are what enables you to interact with crystal power. You can soon have these powerful energy points working for you.

CHAKRA POWER

Chakras are energy centres that link the physical and subtle bodies with the environment. Most people know the seven main chakras that run up the spine. However, there are far more chakras (see page 77): two so-called 'minor' ones – the manifestation chakras – are firmly attached to the Earth plane, and are far from minor in their effect. Activating these chakras assists the manifestation process and enhances your ability to project energy out to the material world or to receive it.

ACTIVATING YOUR MANIFESTATION CHAKRAS

The manifestation chakras are located in the centre of your palms. If you rub your hands together briskly and then bring them together with the fingers steepled and the palms apart, you can feel these chakras tingling and pulsating – almost as though there is a ball of energy between your palms.

Fully functioning manifestation chakras help you to receive energy from the universe – or from crystals – and channel this into your energy field. They also assist in putting your intention out to the universe. Your creativity flows – it is a magnetic, energetic process of attraction and expression.

HOW TO OPEN THE MANIFESTATION CHAKRAS

1 State your intention of opening the two manifestation chakras in your palms.

2 Rapidly open and close your fingers five or six times.

3 Concentrate your attention into your right-hand palm and then into your left-hand one (if you are left-handed, reverse this process). Picture the chakras opening like petals. The centres will become hot and energized.

4 Bring your hands together. Stop as soon as you feel the energy of the two chakras meeting.

5 If you brought your hands together with the fingers touching, reverse them now so that your hands are pointing in opposite directions. Place your right and then your left hand above the other. You'll soon learn to recognize what works for you. With a little practice you'll be able to open the chakras simply by focusing your attention there.

6 Place a crystal-point on your hand (see left). Feel the energies radiating into your palm. Turn the point toward your arm and then toward your fingers. Sense the direction of the energy flow. Crystal-points channel energy in the direction that they face. Rounded crystals radiate energy equally in all directions.

KEEPING YOUR CRYSTALS WORKING FOR YOU

Crystals pick up negative energy very quickly and must be kept cleansed and dedicated to your purpose. If you are using them for manifestation, it is sensible to ensure that you are the only person who handles them. This means placing them somewhere where they will not be disturbed.

CLEANSING YOUR CRYSTALS

When you have chosen your crystal, it needs to be cleansed and dedicated, as it will almost certainly have lost energy during mining and transportation, and may well have picked up negative vibrations from other potential purchasers. If you are using a crystal of your own, cleansing it ensures that you start afresh. You also need to cleanse a stone after healing, as it will have absorbed energetic toxins.

The simplest way to cleanse a crystal or faceted gem is to hold it under running water for a few moments and then place it in the sun to re-energize. You can also place it in brown rice overnight or use a proprietary crystal cleanser. Porous or friable crystals may be damaged by water, so they are best placed in the sun on clear Quartz or Carnelian for a few hours. White or clear crystals also enjoy being left out in the moonlight overnight to recharge, or you can place them on a windowsill.

ACTIVATING YOUR CRYSTALS

When the crystal is cleansed and re-energized, hold it in your hands for a few moments and open your manifestation chakras (see page 30) to connect to its power. Dedicate it to your highest good. Picture it surrounded by light (or place it in front of a candle, if you find visualizing difficult). Now clearly state your intention for the crystal (see page 22). Do this with all your crystals before starting your manifesting.

STORING YOUR CRYSTALS

Tumbled stones can be stored together in a bag, but delicate crystals should be wrapped separately and kept in a box when not in use, to avoid scratching them. Adding a Carnelian to your bag or box ensures that your stones are always cleansed and energized, ready for use. If other people handle your crystals, remember to cleanse them afterwards.

PART TWO

Manifesting with crystals

All ancient civilizations honoured and venerated stone, but also used it for more pragmatic purposes to shape their world – it was their technology, after all. You too can take advantage of the ancient power imbued within stones to manifest the life you want. Honour your crystals, respect them and they will reward you with all that you desire. All you need to add is your intention and your gratitude. In the pages that follow you will discover ways to harness the power of stones to enhance all aspects of your life.

The secret of manifesting

The secret of good manifesting is knowing yourself, recognizing who you are at your core and expressing that out to the world. To do this, you have to strip off the layers of conditioning, the toxic emotions and background thoughts that have been overlaid on your pure self – whether these are personal, ancestral or cultural. You must transform them into beliefs that support, rather than sabotage, your manifesting. Taking time out to meditate quietly, and to meet your core self without judgment or conditions, is repaid again and again with perfect manifestation. Recognizing that, at your core, you are an all-powerful being of light and joy is one of the greatest gifts you can give yourself. As is counting your blessings and feeling gratitude for what you have, rather than focusing on what you don't have. Both of these gifts reflect out to the world an expectation that your needs are met, which in turn draws back to you a cornucopia of good things. Dispassionate detachment from the outcome of your objectives is another gift to yourself. If you have an emotional investment in the outcome – that is, if you judge yourself by the success or failure of achieving what you think you most desire – then your manifestation is doomed to fail from the start. Emotional investment is different from emotional involvement. If you are emotionally involved in the initial manifesting process, feeling all the joyful intensity of being in its flow, this facilitates manifestation. But emotional investment in the result blocks the flow, because it demands that the outcome is exactly what you envisage – which may not be for your highest good. So learning to let go is yet another manifesting secret, as is being open to receive. If you can be comfortable with the idea that what you so desperately desire may not be the thing you actually need, then you open up your life to serendipitous synchronicity stepping in.

- Relax
- let go
- stop worrying
- be positive
- accept
            …and all is revealed.

MANIFESTATION QUARTZ
The great manifestor

The essence of a manifestation crystal is 'As you think, so you are. As you are in your heart, so is your world.' It reminds you that it is the thoughts, aspirations, attitudes and fundamental beliefs that lurk unsuspected deep within your subconscious mind that shape your world and create the self-fulfilling prophecies by which you live. Meditate with a Manifestation Quartz to transform your core self.

UNDERSTANDING THIS CRYSTAL

This Quartz formation has a small, perfectly formed crystal enfolded within an outer crystal. It illustrates that your core self inhabits a 'bubble of reality' that moves with you wherever you go. A Manifestation Quartz teaches you how to align effortlessly to the manifestation process. It amplifies and enhances your intentions, thoughts, feelings and beliefs – positive or negative. If you fear lack, this is what you experience. But if you expect abundance, this is what you receive. This crystal helps you to recognize all your blessings, no matter how small. If the inner crystal is contained within Amethyst, Smoky Quartz or Citrine, it adds the properties of that crystal to the manifestation process. Amethyst assists spiritual manifestation, Smoky Quartz grounds it into the everyday world and Citrine enhances abundance at every level.

Manifestation Quartz asks you to dig deep and discover whether you truly believe you deserve what you seek. If not, other crystals may be needed to shift your core beliefs to positive ones. It also asks whether you are ready to receive what you have requested – and whether you understand all the ramifications. It is a crystal of right timing and may, if you are prepared to listen, suggest a more soul-focused timetable or even a different outcome.

MANIFESTATION QUARTZ AND MANIFESTATION

A formation that facilitates visualization, this is the perfect crystal with which to meditate to connect to your inner life. If there is ambivalence over what you seek, or conflict between what your soul-plan and your ego want, the crystal highlights this. Activate it to bring you all that your heart desires. This stone works best if you seek to manifest in a spirit of cooperation and generosity, for the good of all. It does not support purely selfish or self-centred requests. Use it to contemplate your inner desires and to identify the exact nature of your intention. Spending a few quiet moments with your Manifestation Quartz helps you to define precisely the wording for affirmations or statements of intent, before activating your crystal.

USING MANIFESTATION QUARTZ

A manifestation crystal facilitates specific focus and knowing who you are at your core. Meditate with one in order to meet your core self. An excellent crystal for creative group work, it assists in manifesting solutions or enhancing community-centred activities. Visualize what you wish for and feel intensely what it is like to have it, so that the intensity flows into the crystal, which can be set up on a manifestation altar as a reminder.

Alternative crystals

GENERATOR FORMATION

A Generator takes two forms and may be any type of Quartz, including Amethyst, Spirit or Smoky Quartz. It is either a cluster with points radiating out in all directions or a large point with six equal-sided faces meeting in a point in the middle. Generators, as the name suggests, create energy and radiate it out to the world around you. If you are using a Generator cluster, each point can be activated for a specific purpose. It is often used to manifest healing.

GENERATOR FORMATION

JADE, CITRINE, AMMOLITE

Jade and Citrine traditionally generate abundance and attract good fortune. Ammolite is known as the Seven Colour Prosperity Stone because of its opalized flashes of colour. Green supports entrepreneurship, while yellow attracts wealth and orange attracts creativity.

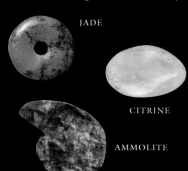

JADE

CITRINE

AMMOLITE

MANIFESTATION QUARTZ ACTIVATION
Generating inner wealth

Crystals need to be activated to set them working. Once your Generator has been activated, you can set up a manifestation altar or place it in the wealth corner of your home to kick-start the manifestation process into action. Setting up a manifestation altar reminds you of your intention and constantly radiates it out to the world. It is a way of honouring your blessings, not a way of worshipping money. It connects you to your inner wealth and the resources you have, and reminds you to express gratitude on a daily basis. Use it wisely for an abundant life. You will need, in addition to your Manifestation Quartz, a cloth, some flowers, a candle and any other objects for your altar.

1 Cleanse your crystal (see page 33), then hold it in your hands and connect to its power, feeling it radiating into your manifestation chakras (see page 30) and throughout your whole being.

2 Say out loud, 'I dedicate this crystal to the highest good of all and to activating a positive manifestation process in my life.' If you have a specific manifesting purpose in mind, state it.

3 Extend your left arm out to its full extent, holding your manifesting crystal as you do so. Bend your right arm at the elbow. Bring your hand up to your forehead over your third eye. Hold that pose for a few moments as your desires wing their way into physical manifestation.

4 Choose a place where you will see your manifestation altar daily, but where it will not be disturbed. The wealth corner of your home is ideal, but you can place it elsewhere. The wealth corner is the rear left-hand corner diagonally furthest from the front door of your home, or the back left-hand

corner of a room. It is part of the Chinese Feng Shui system, but anyone can take advantage of its auspiciousness. If there is no room for an altar, put your crystal in the wealth corner – even the smallest crystal works wonders. A cloth is useful to delineate your sacred space: gold is often used as this is a colour of abundance, but you could choose green to ground your manifesting into the physical world, red to activate your creativity, blue to stimulate your spirituality, and so on.

5 Place your Manifestation Quartz in the centre of the altar. On one side you may like to place some fresh flowers and on the other a candle. If you are manifesting something specific, place around the crystal photographs or objects that symbolize your intention. If you have a Generator Formation, you can add this too.

6 Light the candle and quietly focus your attention on the altar. Joyously experience within yourself how it feels to have already all the inner and outer resources that you need. Hold the intensity of feeling in the moment with all your attention, and then let it go. Blow out the candle and send your manifesting intention out with the smoke.

7 Remember to keep your altar cleansed and the flowers fresh. You can light the candle daily to keep your intention active and focused. Each time you do so, say, 'Thank you for the blessings I receive daily. I am grateful for the abundance of this world and my inner self.'

Stepping into your power

Used wisely, power is constructive, life-enhancing and empowering. It gives you true inner authority, clarity and total freedom. Stepping into your power adds joy and authentic meaning to your life. It heightens your senses and deepens your perspicacity. Power is an instinctual knowing. Wise use of your power helps you to draw on inner resources to shape and enrich your life – it nourishes you and affirms your pathway. When you are empowered, you feel secure enough to risk opening yourself up, signing up to life and growing. It gives you the impetus and courage to take those essential first steps. Personal empowerment stimulates your creativity and power of attraction, and the willpower to manifest what you seek. You come to realize the extraordinary power of your own thoughts. When you are empowered, you are congruent: your thoughts, beliefs and actions match. You radiate inner power. This leads others to treat you with respect, as they recognize someone who can be trusted at a very deep level. Above all, when you are empowered, you follow your passion and live your bliss.

Power is often confused with control. It has been defined as 'the ability or capacity to perform or act effectively' and 'strength or force exerted, or capable of being exerted'. But it is much more than this. Rather than having control over something or exerting force, it is the power to shape the world effortlessly around you. It is the power to *allow* – to let life move through you so that the universe can bring you all that you seek.

The most common way to lose your power is to not have realized that you had any in the first place. So the first step to regaining your power is self-awareness – letting go of the self-limiting beliefs that hold you back. The second step is to find your vision: to recognize what is possible in your life, the skills that you already possess and those that you need to develop. When you live your vision with passion, your life is meaningful, fulfilling and true. It is empowerment in action.

MALACHITE
Your true power crystal

Malachite teaches that when you're fully empowered, you manifest your own reality. But it points out that, if you're not standing in your power, you are unable to manifest anything except negativity. This stone brings to the surface all the hidden issues, toxic thoughts and repressed feelings that are holding you back or sabotaging you. Once you have faced these feelings, you can reclaim your power.

UNDERSTANDING THIS CRYSTAL

A resolute stone that draws insights up from the subconscious mind, Malachite is the raw essence of copper. Its protective influence guards and guides you on your journey through the underworld and all that resides there, takes you through death of the ego and your old self and facilitates the regeneration of your true self. As the crystal is itself evolving, it is the perfect stone for all transmutational shadow work, especially on an emotional and intellectual level. And the more you work with it, the more expansive its influence becomes.

Malachite's convoluted whorls help to illuminate all the hidden corners of your mind. It brings to light the inner critic, or the saboteur who trips up your manifestation intentions. This stone demands that you take a hard look at the causes – both karmic and psychosomatic (toxic emotions manifesting as a physical condition) – that lie behind an apparent inability to manifest ease and wellbeing. It facilitates release and letting go, so that you can move forward. Malachite draws off negativity at all levels, releasing ancient trauma and outgrown feelings so that you find deep emotional healing. Working with this crystal brings you face-to-face with whatever is blocking your spiritual path and assists in its transmutation.

MALACHITE AND MANIFESTATION

Malachite offers you the gift of taking responsibility for yourself and your actions. It helps you to break ties with the past and reprogramme your expectations by teaching that you need to be aware of each thought and emotion that passes through every level of your being, as each has consequences. It is the perfect stone to assist in letting go of old ego-identity and everything that restricts your sense of true self. With Malachite's assistance, you can step into your true power and from there manifest your own reality. This stone will surprise you with the depth of transmutation that you can achieve – and the evasive distractions that have been holding you back. Face up to your secrets and, with Malachite's assistance, you can manifest your truly powerful self.

USING MALACHITE

Malachite is particularly useful when you are seeking to manifest a way out of trauma and emotional drama. It brings into the light secrets, deceptions and sabotage by your self and others. But you can use it in any area of your life to call on your power, to be strong and resolute, and to manifest the real you. *Always use Malachite in its polished form, and wash your hands after use.*

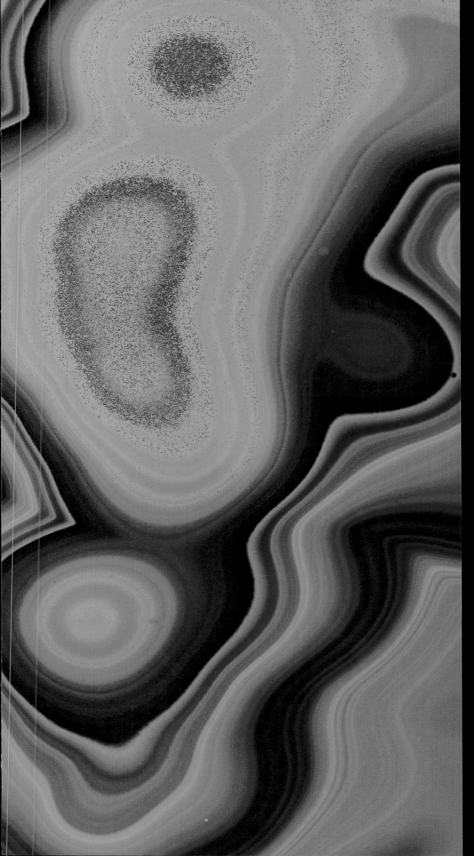

Alternative crystals

APACHE TEAR, RAINBOW OBSIDIAN, MAHOGANY OBSIDIAN

If you don't have Malachite to hand, you can use Obsidian – preferably in the form of a gentle Apache Tear, tender Rainbow or soft Mahogany Obsidian – as this stone helps you to surface and release deeply held emotional blockages and taboo feelings. The effect of pure Black Obsidian can be powerfully cathartic, so having the support of Rhodochrosite, Rose Quartz or Mangano Calcite (stones of forgiveness) placed over your heart helps to bring the letting-go process to a successful conclusion.

APACHE TEAR

MAHOGANY OBSIDIAN

RAINBOW OBSIDIAN

BLUE SCAPOLITE, SMOKY QUARTZ

If you need an alternative stone when meeting your inner critic or saboteur, Blue Scapolite acts as an effective introduction, as it helps you to renegotiate with your less-constructive inner figures, as does Smoky Quartz.

SMOKY QUARTZ

BLUE SCAPOLITE

MALACHITE MEDITATION
What am I holding on to?

This Malachite meditation is a potent way to connect with the issues
that are keeping you from stepping into your power. We may think that
past issues are resolved and that the path ahead is clear, but often old
hurts and confusion lie buried, acting as energetic blocks to our progress.
Malachite's strong protective properties help you to feel safe as you
gently let go of old thoughts, feelings and experiences that no longer
serve you (as well as the inner figures that have tripped you up) and
open up to the wisdom they offer. Take as long as you need for this
process of release.

1 Settle yourself comfortably where you will not be
disturbed, and breathe gently, withdrawing your
attention from the outside world and into the crystal.
Keep your eyes half-open and gaze at the whorls
and contours of your Malachite as you connect with
the power of the crystal. Feel its strength in your
hand. Let its energy radiate up your arms and into
your heart and mind. As you focus on each whorl,
let it take you inward. Allow the bands to move you
gently into contact with your deepest self. Close
your eyes and relax. When you feel ready, place the
crystal over your solar plexus.

2 Ask the crystal to let you know what you are
holding onto, and what it would be beneficial to
release. Notice any thoughts that drift into your
mind; recognize if there is a pattern, then let them
go with love. Acknowledge any emotions that arise,
and lovingly release them. Take your mind around
your body to any areas of tension or pain, breathe
gently and let them go. Let the Malachite show
you any hooks that are in your heart and gently
dissolve them, filling their place with loving energy
and forgiveness.

3 Ask the Malachite to show you how the past is affecting your present in any area of your life, and how your mind and your emotions control what you manifest. Willingly surrender all that no longer serves you – all the pain and emotions, beliefs, expectations, experiences or inner figures that have weighed you down and held you back. Acknowledge them and let them be drawn into the crystal for transmutation. Let them go, with forgiveness in your heart

4 Ask the crystal to show you the gifts hidden behind that old pain, the qualities you have developed and the resources you can draw on. Step into your power. Allow yourself to know how you will use them, and how you will work with this crystal in future to manifest your new reality.

5 Ask your Malachite if it has any other information, and wait quietly for the answer. If an inner figure appears, negotiate a positive role for it.

6 Before you begin the return journey, put your attention out to the subtle bodies around your physical self, and ask the crystal to draw off and transmute any negative energies or disharmonies that have not yet been released, bringing all the subtle bodies into alignment.

7 Feel the strong protection from the Malachite wrapping around you. Finally, feel the strength of the crystal and its powerful connection to the Earth, grounding you into your physical existence, bringing you fully into the present moment. When you feel ready, thank the crystal, open your eyes, get up and move around.

De-cluttering your mind

Ninety per cent of our thoughts are unnecessary, unfocused, unconscious and destructive – until we de-clutter our minds and take control of our thought processes. Getting into the habit of monitoring your thoughts at each and every moment is essential if you are to manifest at the highest, most productive level. But if this level of mindfulness sounds too much, practise it for a few moments every hour or so – setting an alarm that rings is helpful. Simply stop what you are doing when the alarm sounds and monitor your mind. Get into the habit of jotting your thoughts down – either mentally or on paper. Take a few moments to clear your head, then ask yourself, 'Is this thought true?', 'Is it helpful?', 'Is it mine?' You may be surprised at how many of your thoughts don't actually belong to you or are no longer true. Cross them off the list. Transform these limiting beliefs and you will transform your world.

Typical limiting beliefs:
- I can only be happy if I have money.
- I'd have to work incredibly hard to be prosperous.
- It's not my fault.
- I can never get out of this pit.
- It's imperative that I …
- There'll never be enough.
- Money is the root of all evil.
- The world owes me a living.
- I won't be loved/approved of if I do that.
- It's not safe to take a risk.
- I'll always be in debt.
- I don't deserve …
- I'm not good enough.
- People like me can't do that.
- There's virtue in poverty.
- It's vulgar to be rich.
- Following my dream will mean that I'll always be poor.
- I can't turn my passion into a career – it's not feasible.
- I have to be realistic; I can't …
- I don't have the right accent or background to do that kind of a job.
- I didn't go to the right kind of school or college.
- I can't help it – it's my karma.

Ask yourself how many times each day you say something similar. Recognize how this limits your manifesting opportunities, and resolve to change it.

RUTILATED QUARTZ
Your purification crystal

Rutilated Quartz is an effective purifier and integrator of energy. It encourages letting go, helps you to clear your mind and teaches you how to sharpen your focus, open your higher mind and gain profound insight. It instils clarity and promotes your spiritual growth. This crystal helps you to de-clutter your mind of limiting beliefs and background thoughts that would otherwise sabotage your manifestation.

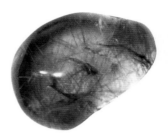

UNDERSTANDING THIS CRYSTAL

The fine strands within Rutilated Quartz comprise the reddish-brown mineral known as rutile, which imparts an ethereal vibration that encourages attunement to the divine and to the multi-dimensions of being. This crystal draws cosmic light down to Earth to stimulate creativity and manifest a more spiritually attuned way of being. Nevertheless, Rutilated Quartz is a pragmatic crystal that goes to the heart of a matter and insists that you deal with it. It helps you to purify toxic thoughts and release constricting emotions, replacing them with a positive outlook. You cannot evade issues with this crystal. It brings to the surface previous life causes, implanted beliefs and destructive thought patterns, and shows you where they have tripped you up in the past. Teaching that you manifest what you are, this crystal enables you to truly understand the power of thought.

Rutilated Quartz lifts your spirits. Working with cell membranes and synapses to switch on beneficial DNA potential and switch off destructive patterns, it heals cellular memory and stabilizes the energetic meridians of your body, to support a new way of being. Dissolving anxiety and helping overcome your fears, it facilitates change to a more positive, self-supporting belief system with constructive thoughts that literally create a new world.

RUTILATED QUARTZ AND MANIFESTATION

Rutilated Quartz connects you to your soul-plan and helps you to understand the effects of previous actions and ingrained patterns. It helps you to distinguish between karma as 'payback for previous actions' and your soul intention. So, for instance, if you live a life of lack because of a previous vow of poverty or a life of greed, it helps you to release from this. But if you have taken on a particular way of life as a learning experience, it assists you in gaining the most from this. If you took on that life of lack in order to stimulate recognition of your inner resources, for example, it reminds you to look within and find your strengths.

USING RUTILATED QUARTZ

Meditating with this crystal, or using it in layouts, helps you to focus your mind constructively. When placed over the chakras, Rutilated Quartz activates the energetic power rods that link your physical being to subtle dimensions. One of its major benefits is amplifying the power of your thoughts so that they are projected out to the universe as solid, tangible beams of creative energy that draw back to you whatever you seek. This crystal encourages you to share what you have and to be magnanimous in your desires.

Alternative crystals

TOURMALINATED QUARTZ, BLACK TOURMALINE, SELENITE, SMOKY QUARTZ

If Rutilated Quartz is not available, use Tourmalinated Quartz, or a mix of Black Tourmaline and Selenite or Smoky Quartz. Crystals containing Tourmaline are natural detoxifiers of mental energy, drawing off negativity and blocking the implanted thoughts of other people, so that you stand in your own thought-power. When you add Selenite or Quartz to the mix, cosmic light is drawn in to transmute your mundane mind into higher understanding.

TOURMALINATED QUARTZ

BLACK TOURMALINE

SELENITE

SMOKY QUARTZ

BERYL

Beryl is useful when you have followed someone else's mental imperative. It helps you to focus on doing only what you need to do for your own highest good – facilitating the shedding of emotional or mental baggage that has been holding you back, and manifesting your own potential.

BERYL

RUTILATED QUARTZ PLACEMENT

How do I clear my mind?

This layout enables you to de-clutter your mind and change your mental blueprint. Many of our core beliefs have been implanted either by personal or cultural past experience, or by people such as parents and teachers. Once your mind has been de-cluttered, you can replace negativity with core beliefs that support your manifesting. Self-esteem, trusting in the universe while taking responsibility for yourself, and going with the flow all facilitate the process. Return to this layout and the beliefs it transmutes as often as necessary, until you can catch a destructive thought before it has time to make itself felt. Make mindfulness your way of life. You will need six Rutilated Quartz tumbled stones or small points, plus a larger point.

1 Sit quietly holding your large Rutilated Quartz and connect to the power of the stone. Review the background thoughts that were revealed when you monitored your mind (see page 49). Look at all those toxic thoughts that were implanted in childhood and at the ones that you have acquired since, or that you have recognized as past-life programmes or vows that need reframing. Think about each negative belief. Where possible, trace it back to its source. Ask yourself if it was true then, and whether you believe it now. If it is no longer true, release the thought into the large Rutilated Quartz for transmutation, saying the opposite belief as you do so – a positive to replace the negative. Do this for each of your limiting beliefs and negative thoughts. Remember to ask yourself if you are open to receiving abundance in all its forms.

2 Resolve to change permanently the thought pattern that was not beneficial for your wellbeing. Lay out a stone at each point of a downward-facing triangle, using three of your smaller Rutilated Quartz stones. Link the triangle up in your mind. This represents all those negative thoughts that you have laid to rest.

3 Over that triangle lay crystals at the points of an upward-facing triangle. Join up the triangle in your mind. This represents all the positive beliefs that you are building into your new mental blueprint – one that is abundant and prosperous and leaves room for good things to manifest and enrich your life.

4 Place your large Rutilated Quartz in the centre of the Star of David, so that the transmutation process can continue. Feel it radiating cosmic light and love into the surrounding crystal layout and into your daily life.

5 This layout makes a perfect focus for a five-minute daily meditation. Gaze at it, letting your eyes go out of focus and quietening your breathing while you observe the crystals. If you become aware of yet another limiting belief, let it go into the central crystal, and state out loud the opposite, life-enhancing belief. Do not try to make anything happen; simply allow. Notice how different you feel after a week: how clear and focused your mind is and how much sharper your power of thought. Cleanse your Rutilated Quartz regularly.

Clearing your karma

Karma states that 'what goes around comes around', but this does not have to be a negative concept. We may generate 'good' karma just as easily as 'bad' karma, and the process is one of balance rather than punishment. It is part of our soul-growth, but we can move beyond our karma into an enlightened state of being in which we recognize that we create our reality in each and every moment. Clearing your karma is another of the keys to manifestation.

You don't have to believe in previous lives to believe in karma. You can simply accept that 'what goes around comes around'. Earlier in your present life or ingrained ancestral patterns can represent the 'before' that creates your karma. However, if you do understand the concept in its fullest breadth, you recognize that your soul is on a much longer and more purposeful journey than is traditionally conceived in the West. The wider picture behind apparent failures in the manifestation process is then revealed, as is the key to unlocking the future.

Your soul has a plan for your life, an agenda that is set before you incarnate. It may focus around ingrained patterns that you intended to change, or new resources and learning that you seek. However, once incarnated in a physical body, you tend to forget such plans, and conditioning kicks in – until you recognize the pattern and change it. The soul may block plans that are destructive or not for your highest good, although you do have free will; but it may allow learning to continue, as a lesson in what happens when you step off the soul's path. You may also get caught up in karmic imperatives that override your soul-plan. The major karmic causes are soul-contracts, pacts, vows, promises, expectations and debts set up in previous lives, which may require releasing or reframing in order to come into line with your current soul-evolution plan. Fortunately, the karma of grace allows us to make adjustments and step into another dimension of being – one where we consciously manifest our own reality.

WIND FOSSIL AGATE
Your karmic transformer

Wind Fossil Agate teaches that you are an eternal soul incarnated as a human being at this moment in time. It reveals the karmic and emotional baggage that you carry with you, and the defences that you erected to ensure your survival. Gently peeling away the layers that hide who you are at your core, it reveals the beauty of your soul – the soul that has the power to manifest infinite possibilities.

UNDERSTANDING THIS CRYSTAL

An enduring stone carrying the karma of grace, Wind Fossil Agate symbolizes layers scoured first by water and then by strong winds blowing through desert canyons, leaving the tougher portion prominently displayed. The stone knows what it is to go through the fires of transmutation to reach its beautiful core, and thus helps you to reveal who you truly are.

Wind Fossil Agate scours away the karmic encrustations and emotional baggage carried across eons of time by your soul. It also knows the survival skills that are necessary to adapt during life on Earth – it has changed its form over its long lifetime. If there is anything from the past left to reshape or face up to, Wind Fossil Agate will help you to resolve this so that you can move on. This crystal also helps you to identify soul-lessons yet to be learned, gifts that have gone unrecognized, and promises, situations and relationships that have passed their sell-by date and need reframing.

WIND FOSSIL AGATE AND MANIFESTATION

Wind Fossil Agate reveals all the karmic causes that lie behind apparent mis-manifestation or a seeming inability to manifest what you need. It highlights the expectations built up from past experiences, and helps you to release your judgment of how the future will be, based on those expectations. It also shows you the karmic strengths that you have to draw on, the survival skills you have developed and the endless possibilities of your soul. It reassures you that you will survive, no matter what; but, in releasing the past, it opens up the probability of manifesting a bright future in the here and now.

USING WIND FOSSIL AGATE

Meditating with Wind Fossil Agate – especially on the past-life chakras behind the ears (see page 58) – shows you the soul-contracts, pacts and promises that must be left behind, and also points the way forward. The stone assists deep regression to reframe previous lives, although this should be undertaken under the guidance of a qualified past life therapist.

This crystal is particularly helpful if carried during traumatic or challenging situations, where strength and endurance are needed to overcome circumstances over which you seemingly have no control, as it draws on your karmic survival strengths. Wind Fossil Agate knows the secret of right timing. It offers the confidence that is needed to wait quietly until the moment for change arrives, and the courage to make the move.

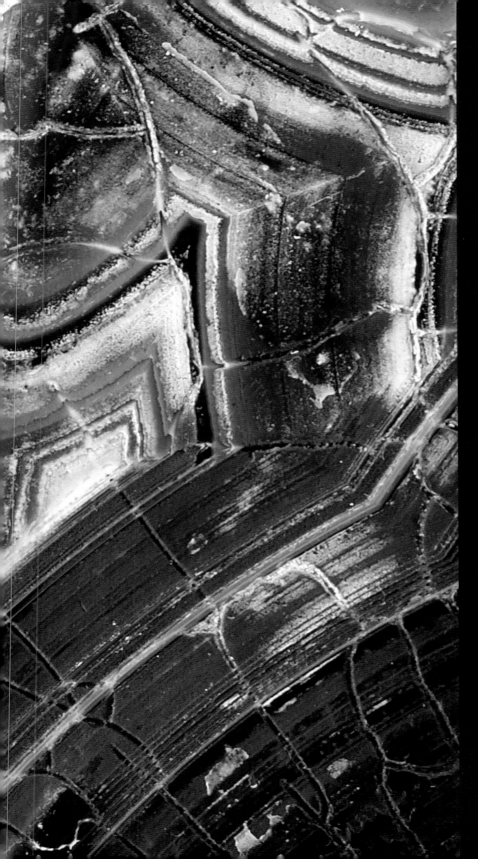

Alternative crystals

DUMORTIERITE, BLIZZARD STONE

Dumortierite (a form of blue Quartz) and Blizzard Stone (a form of Gabbro) stimulate memories, when placed on the past-life chakras. These stones help to maintain a dispassionate focus and to recognize the soul-gifts and lessons in your experiences. They also make you more receptive to soul-guidance. Use Dumortierite if you suffer from a sense of lack in your life. Blizzard Stone assists in erasing memories of persecution or prejudice.

DUMORTIERITE   BLIZZARD STONE

GOLDEN HEALER, RAINBOW MAYANITE

Beautiful ethereal Golden Healer and sparkling Rainbow Mayanite – an even higher-vibration crystal – heal the subtle layers of the biomagnetic body that hold ancient memories, etheric scars and karmic patterns. Gently dissolving these, the crystals infill the spaces with cosmic light, manifesting a new soul-potential.

GOLDEN HEALER   RAINBOW MAYANITE

WIND FOSSIL AGATE ACTIVATION

How do I clear my karma?

The past-life chakras are situated behind your ears and along the bony ridge at the base of your skull. These chakras hold memories of your past and deeply ingrained patterns set up over many lifetimes, as well as the karmic gifts, skills and wisdom that can assist your present life. Massaging these chakras may trigger flashbacks, but it assists in letting go of anything from the past that is interfering with your manifesting. Cleansing these chakras is particularly helpful if you have made vows of poverty in the past, or soul-pacts or promises that are preventing you from moving forward now in your life.

1 Cleanse your Wind Fossil Agate by leaving it overnight in brown rice. Throw the rice away afterwards; do not eat it.

2 Hold your crystal lightly in your hands and connect to the power of the stone – feel it radiating throughout your whole being. Dedicate it to removing all the limiting karma, pacts, promises, soul-contracts, vows, expectations and ingrained patterns from the past, whenever that may have been, and to revealing your karmic credits and the wisdom of your soul.

3 Close your eyes. Using whichever hand is most comfortable, place your Wind Fossil Agate behind your right ear and gently massage along the bony ridge of your skull until you reach the hollow at the back. Begin behind the left ear and massage to the centre again. As you work, remind yourself that you are scouring away all the karmic encrustations to reveal who you truly are. Continue to massage for as long as feels appropriate. If any memories arise, watch them objectively, gaining insights into what has been holding you back or recognizing the karmic strengths you have developed. If the memory is negative, do not judge or blame; simply watch and accept that that was how it was then, but remind yourself that it is different now. If any reframing is required, do it now. If, for instance, you find that you have made a vow or promise that no longer serves you, add 'For that life only'. If beliefs such as 'There'll never be enough' were implanted, change them to 'There is always enough'. If someone is holding you to something that is no longer relevant, or if you feel guilty and responsible for someone else, let that go. Negotiate with the other person if

necessary –Wind Fossil Agate helps you to know instinctively what to say. If you recognize a detrimental pattern, wipe it out and replace it with a beneficial one. Be creative in your reframing: change the scenario entirely, if that is appropriate. Now thank the memories for showing themselves and let them go, with love and forgiveness. Remind yourself that that was then, and this is now. Willingly embrace your karmic credits and the lessons you have learned.

4 Holding your Wind Fossil Agate, say out loud, 'I release any vows, pacts, promises, soul-contracts, implanted thoughts, emotional baggage, detrimental patterns or beliefs, outdated soul-imperatives, and anything else that is standing in the way of manifesting my true self.' 'Comb' the Wind Fossil Agate all around your body at arm's length, being sure to include your back and around your feet. You may feel quite chilly at this point, but allow everything detrimental to fall away and reveal your karmic gifts.

5 Hold the Wind Fossil Agate above your head. Invite in the karma of grace and feel your whole body being suffused with cosmic light and filling all the spaces where you let go.

6 Ask the crystal to show you your soul in all its beauty, so that you manifest it fully and create your own reality.

7 Picture a bubble of protection all around you and a root going deep down into the Earth to anchor you into incarnation. Put your crystal down and step into the present as it manifests in each and every moment. Cleanse your crystal.

Creating abundance

Abundance is an attitude of mind. It is so much more than just having money. A strong inner sense of abundant wellbeing opens your mind to infinite possibilities. Abundance means living in a deeply enriched way – physically, mentally, emotionally and spiritually. It is founded upon valuing yourself and your life exactly as you are *right now*. So often people exist in a void of waiting before they begin to live, instead of living in the moment. But it doesn't have to be like that. You have all the riches you need within yourself to create an abundant world. You just need to believe it. An unshakeable sense of your own inner worth is the greatest resource you can develop. Honour yourself for what you have achieved. Be compassionate toward yourself. Feel blessed, and trust that you can manifest all that you require and generously share what you have with others. This creates a never-ending flow. You live in an abundant world.

Remember: 'like follows like':
- What your mind conceives, it achieves – so think positively.
- Measure your self-worth by who you are, not what you own.
- Focus on exactly what you wish to attract, not on what you don't have.
- Follow your bliss: do what you love.
- Be grateful and feel blessed.
- Believe that you can bring your dreams to fruition.
- Accept and appreciate the small joys of everyday life.
- Avoid doubt, guilt and procrastination; let go of fear and self-pity.
- Share what you have, and take pleasure in giving.

CITRINE
Your abundance crystal

Citrine teaches you how to live abundantly and shows you what true prosperity is. With its zingy, joyous energy it is particularly beneficial for attracting abundance into your life and for dissolving blockages to creativity. This enthusiastic stone carries the power of the sun, energizing and stimulating on all levels. Work with this stone and you will instinctively put out what you most wish to attract. Use it if you seek to boost your self-esteem. Keeping a Citrine in your purse or pocket means that you'll never be without resources.

UNDERSTANDING THIS CRYSTAL

An exceedingly beneficial stone, Citrine is a form of Quartz and therefore amplifies and regenerates energy. Most of the golden-yellow or brownish-yellow Citrine sold today is heat-treated Amethyst or Smoky Quartz, which carries the forces of transmutation and inner alchemy. Having been through the fires of transmutation itself, it accompanies you through all the dark places of life and brings you safely out the other side, encouraging you to recognize the gifts in your experience.

Citrine is an extremely helpful stone in situations where you need to gain insight or confidence before you can manifest change, or where doubt or self-destructive behaviour is holding you back. Its bright yellow colour is like a ray of sunshine coming into your life, and it's impossible to remain depressed around this irrepressible crystal.

Natural Citrine is rare, but exceedingly potent. Light, bright natural Citrine activates your self-confidence and helps you to recognize your own worth, while natural Smoky Citrine (Kundalini Quartz) carries Kundalini power – an inner, subtle, creative, spiritual and sexual energy that resides at the base of the spine – which enhances your passion and facilitates you becoming the co-creator of your world. Its energy is so bright that you naturally attract passion and power, because negativity cannot hold sway.

CITRINE AND MANIFESTATION

Citrine draws toward you an abundance of opportunity, friendship, good health, inner wealth and outer riches. It is the perfect stone to use whenever you wish to stimulate passion or greater joy, or to enhance your creativity, but it also assists in attracting the perfect job, a pay-rise or a new home.

Encouraging you to share what you have with others, Citrine imparts joy to all who work with it. This crystal promotes inner calm, facilitating the emergence of your innate wisdom, and assists the free flow of feelings and emotional balance. Citrine is also perfect when you have been seeking to manifest something for a very long time and don't seem to be getting anywhere. It corrects underlying energy depletion, helps you to recognize and reverse any feelings of lack in your life, and fires up your enthusiasm once again.

USING CITRINE

Citrine is an excellent stone for transmuting energy and radiating positivity. Keep it in your purse or cashbox to generate prosperity.

Alternative crystals

TOPAZ, SUNSTONE

Yellow stones such as bright
Topaz or sunny Sunstone can be
substituted for Citrine, if this stone
is not to hand. They attract to you
all that you wish for and will help
you to maintain an upbeat and
optimistic outlook.

SUNSTONE

TOPAZ

CARNELIAN, CINNABAR, JADE, TURQUOISE

Other traditional stones for creating
abundance are Carnelian, Cinnabar,
Jade and Turquoise, all of which
have thousands of years of historical
use as amulets to support their
manifesting power.

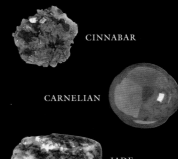

CINNABAR

CARNELIAN

JADE

TURQUOISE

CITRINE RITUAL
How do I create abundance?

Pentangles, or five-pointed stars, naturally draw down universal energy to manifest all that you desire. For this ritual you will need five tumbled or pointed Citrines (if you are using crystals with points, ensure they all face in the appropriate direction in the pentangle). You will also need a gold or green candle, a pen and paper (ideally green or gold paper).

1 Draw a large five-pointed star on your paper with the marker pen.

2 Hold your Citrines in your hands and connect to their power, feeling it radiating into your manifestation chakras. Then, working slowly with focused intent and with your left hand extended, place a Citrine on each point of the star, starting at the top. As you place the stones, see the points of the pentagram joining up and glowing with light.

3 Place your candle in the centre of the star and light it. As you do so, place your right hand to your forehead.

4 Say out loud with focused intent, 'I call the abundant universal energy into my life; let it manifest in everything I do, think, feel or say. So be it.'

5 Feel the universal energy being drawn into the star and radiating out all around you.

6 Quietly contemplate your star for a few moments.

7 When you blow the candle out, feel it sending abundant light into every corner of your being.

8 Dismantle the star and put one of the Citrines in your pocket or purse. Now disconnect your energy and attention from the star and leave the process in motion.

Financial alchemy

Alchemy is the process of turning base metal into gold. In other words, it turns a basic material into a higher, more-refined energetic state. A metaphor for potent psychological change, alchemy is an ancient, transformative process that powered chemistry and metallurgy – and metaphysics. Alchemists spent years in their laboratories seeking the secrets of life. It wasn't just a physical process, for magic was involved too, and the alchemists understood the hidden processes of manifestation and how the manipulation and shaping of energy in the subtle dimensions created a new reality. They also comprehended that as you think, so you are – and that 'as you think' could be transformed. The secret of alchemy was 'As above, so below; as below, so above'. The old alchemists saw a chain of correspondence from the highest to the lowest, which drew down the cosmic powers and returned them in a never-ending cycle. They knew that we are the universe – there is no difference in essence, only in the form that substance takes.

Financial alchemy involves taking something lesser, or seemingly lacking, and manifesting it in a much greater quantity with more value. This does not have to be based purely on money. Financial alchemy encompasses all kinds of wealth, including inner resources, but it can also be used to turn around an ailing company or your own personal finances.

What makes alchemy work:
- Being totally present in the process
- Focused intention
- Holding your centre
- Being non-judgmental
- Trusting in the hidden forces at work
- Filtering, distilling and transmuting the base material into spiritual gold
- Recognizing that you are an integral part of the universe

GOLDSTONE
Your alchemy crystal

Shiny, gem-like Goldstone is created from glass and copper through the process of alchemy, and therefore helps you perform financial alchemy that can transform your life. This crystal is often sold as 'the money stone' and is traditionally used to attract wealth of all kinds. It is also known as the stone of drive and ambition – boosting motivation and the courage to manifest successfully.

UNDERSTANDING THIS CRYSTAL

Goldstone is thought to have first been made in 17th-century Venice by the Miotti, an ancient glass-making family, but is rumoured to have been created long before that by alchemists as they sought to make gold. Another legend says that it was created in Italy by an ancient monastic order, to a jealously guarded secret recipe, and was therefore known as 'monk's gold'.

Created within an alembic (distilling apparatus) in an oxygen-reducing atmosphere, by adding copper or other mineral salts to molten glass, Goldstone was first designated a gemstone in Victorian times. It is popular today for jewellery and for generating wealth. Its sparkling appearance suggests its alternative name of 'stellaria', or star-stone. It is also sometimes called 'Aventurine' and somewhat resembles the natural feldspar crystal of that name, which has long had a reputation as a manifesting crystal and can be substituted for the man-made stone.

GOLDSTONE AND MANIFESTATION

Goldstone is a Generator stone long associated with ambition and drive. Created out of the fires of transmutation, it assists with the introspection that is necessary before you can transform the thought processes that create your external world. It instils

in you the unshakeable self-confidence and positive attitude that enable you to take risks and try something new. When making Goldstone, the molten glass has to be carefully kept at a specific temperature until the mineral salts have crystallized into their spectacular colours. The best-quality Goldstone is found at the heart of the mass when it has cooled, the outer 'shell' being duller and less sparkling. It has to be cracked open and smoothed in order to reveal its beauty. It therefore represents the inner, invisible processes that must occur before visible transmutation can be manifested.

Goldstone helps you to find your inner wealth, and gives you the patience to wait until the timing is exactly right before revealing it. The various colours each have their own particular quality. Blue Goldstone is said to make you luckier with each passing day and to open new opportunities.

USING GOLDSTONE

Goldstone is an excellent stone for prosperity rituals and layouts, as its glittering appearance stimulates the process of 'like attracting like'. When worn as jewellery, it holds an activation well, and retains its transmutative powers and purity of intention over a long period of time. This beautiful stone reminds you of your inner wealth and assists in making the best possible use of your natural resources. Keep one in your pocket or purse.

Alternative crystals

AVENTURINE, JADE

A traditional gambler's talisman and stone of prosperity, Aventurine can be substituted for Goldstone, as can Jade. One of the oldest abundance stones, Jade attracts good fortune to the wearer. It increases the amount of nurturing that you give yourself and protects you from harm; it also transforms negative thoughts into positive ones. Blue-green Jade is useful if you are naturally impatient, as it instils serenity and helps you to wait while the manifesting process unfolds.

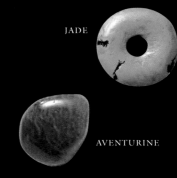

JADE

AVENTURINE

TIGER'S EYE

Tiger's Eye is helpful if you wish to use your power wisely. Combining the energy of the sun with that of the Earth, it brings power down to Earth so that it can be used sensibly, with powerful focus. It was traditionally carried as a talisman against ill-wishing.

TIGER'S EYE

THE GOLDSTONE GRID
How do I create wealth?

Ultimately all your wealth comes from drawing on your own inner resources and manifesting them out into the world. This grid begins by focusing deep within yourself to identify your inner wealth – all the skills and abilities that you can make known. Purifying and removing the dross, it distils them into pure gold. The grid sends these golden qualities out into the world, so that the Law of Attraction comes into play and brings back those qualities magnified one thousand times over. This layout is particularly effective when prepared for at the dark of the moon, which facilitates introspection, and then laid out at the full moon, which facilitates manifestation. You will need ten Goldstones (or Aventurines) for this grid, plus a large sheet of paper (preferably coloured) and a pen or gold marker pen.

1 Hold your Goldstones and connect to their power, feeling it radiating into your manifestation chakras (see page 30). Dedicate them to helping you identify your inner resources and manifesting them out into the world. Hold the stones in your lap with your non-writing hand.

2 Sit quietly with a pen and paper and write down all the resources, skills and abilities that you have, no matter how minor they may seem. Ask yourself, 'What am I keeping hidden? What resources do I have? What riches do I hold at my core? What am I not recognizing about myself?' and allow the answers to rise up into your mind. Note them down. Hold nothing back, and give yourself credit for all your positive qualities.

3 When you have established your qualities, put the list aside and come back to it another day. And another. And another. Add to the list all the things that have risen into your mind since making your original list.

4 Collect together your list of qualities, your large sheet of paper, your gold marker pen and your ten Goldstones. Draw a large counter-clockwise spiral on the paper using the marker pen, beginning at the centre and working outward to end at the top of the page.

5 Starting at the centre, lay your Goldstones along the spiral with your left hand. As you place each stone, acknowledge an inner resource that you have discovered; breathe the quality into the crystal, saying, 'I am wealthy, I have … [name the appropriate quality] and I send this out into the world.' When you have completed the spiral, come back to the centre and touch each stone as you add yet more qualities to the grid.

6 When the grid is fully charged with all the inner qualities you have brought to it, add more qualities that you would like to have, or that would assist the manifestation process.

7 Place your right hand to your forehead. Feel intensely the process of transmutation as the qualities synergize and fly out into the world, to alchemize your inner wealth into outer wealth.

8 Disengage from the process and let the grid do its work.

9 After a week has passed, remove the stones. Draw a clockwise spiral over the top and rearrange the Goldstones to draw toward you all that you need in order to progress your life.

Supporting your health and wellbeing

How you think and feel has a powerful effect on your wellbeing. Your attitude to life ultimately manifests physically. Emotions such as guilt or anger are insidious precursors to dis-ease . Switching to positive thoughts and emotions greatly enhances your ability to remain healthy. But wellbeing is not dependent on physical wellness. It arises out of an inner state of calm-centredness and core stability.

Universal life force, or Qi, flows around your body, passing through subtle meridians (channels) into every organ and cell. Healing crystals contain significant amounts of Qi, which is transferred to your body via your chakras or organs. The chakra system mediates how your energies function, and chakra blockages create dis-ease, but are released by subtle vibrations. Crystals also contain bioscalar waves, which assist with healing and support your immune system. The immune system is your first line of defence and, working efficiently, it keeps you well. If you succumb to infection, a healthy immune system means a faster recovery time. Illnesses such as ME (chronic fatigue syndrome) and viral infections occur when the immune system is underactive; others, such as rheumatoid arthritis and lupus, when it is overactive. Crystals help you to maintain the correct balance. The major healing point for your immune system is the thymus gland (the higher heart chakra, see page 77), located in the centre of the chest. Stimulating this point helps to maintain good health.

Disease may be created in subtle ways. If you receive a shock at the physical, emotional or mental level, your chakras go out of balance and your body reacts. When you are attacked by viruses or by someone's thoughts, dis-ease results. Continual stress or inadequate rest ultimately manifests as physical illness. If you are drained, you have lowered resistance. Chronic anxiety and fear also weaken the body. But research has shown that if you can transmute these toxic experiences into positive ones, intercellular healing will repair the damaged DNA and you will manifest greater health and wellbeing.

QUE SERA
Your health and wellbeing crystal

Que Sera is an amazing healing stone containing a high proportion of Qi and bioscalar waves for optimum health. It helps you to keep your physical body fully energized and in balance, and to understand – and heal – the psychosomatic forces and subtle-energetic disturbances that create dis-ease. It keeps the physical and psychic immune systems working efficiently. With this stone's assistance, you can manifest maximum wellbeing.

UNDERSTANDING THIS CRYSTAL

Born out of the mega-forces that created our universe, Que Sera is a powerful, synergistic combination of minerals with extremely high and yet deeply earthy vibrations. It contains Quartz, Feldspar, Calcite, Kaolinite, Iron, Magnetite, Leucozone and Clinozoisite, all of which have excellent healing properties. This stone does it all: it soothes, energizes, rebalances and restores. Holding it is like being plugged into a major energy socket – it lights up every cell in your body.

Que Sera helps you to tune into the Akashic Record (information on all that has occurred and all that will occur) of your soul's purpose and view all possible outcomes. The stone insists that you stand in your own power. If you have taken on duties or unconsciously assumed a role so that the world perceives you as 'a good person', Que Sera releases you, teaching that such an act of 'service' is actually self-serving. It frees you to be of true selfless service.

With Que Sera there are no mistakes, only learning experiences. If you have a tendency to dwell on problems, this crystal helps you to find constructive solutions and to be confident about your actions. Although the phrase *Que Sera* means 'what will be', with this stone you co-create your own future. (Llanoite contains a stepped-down vibration.)

QUE SERA AND MANIFESTATION

Que Sera acts like a battery to activate your power and manifest wellbeing. It energizes the Earth Star chakra (your link to Mother Earth), the base chakra, sacral chakra and Stellar Gateway chakra (a cosmic portal) and, when placed below the navel, switches on the power-pack that sits in the Dantien atop the sacral chakra, see page 77. With this stone you truly create your own reality.

USING QUE SERA

A powerful carrier of Qi and excellent all-round healer, Que Sera has strong, readily accessible bioscalar-wave energy. A shield against Wi-Fi and other electromagnetic pollutants, it balances and recharges the meridians and organs of the subtle and physical bodies. Place it wherever dis-ease or depletion exists. The crystal activates neurotransmitters to optimize the body's energetic circuit. Que Sera is excellent for the immune system because of its balancing effect. If the immune system is overactive, it sedates; if it is underactive, it stimulates. At the first sign of infection, tape a Que Sera over your thymus. If you find it impossible to say no, keep Que Sera in your pocket. It helps you to say yes only to what is beneficial and for your greater good.

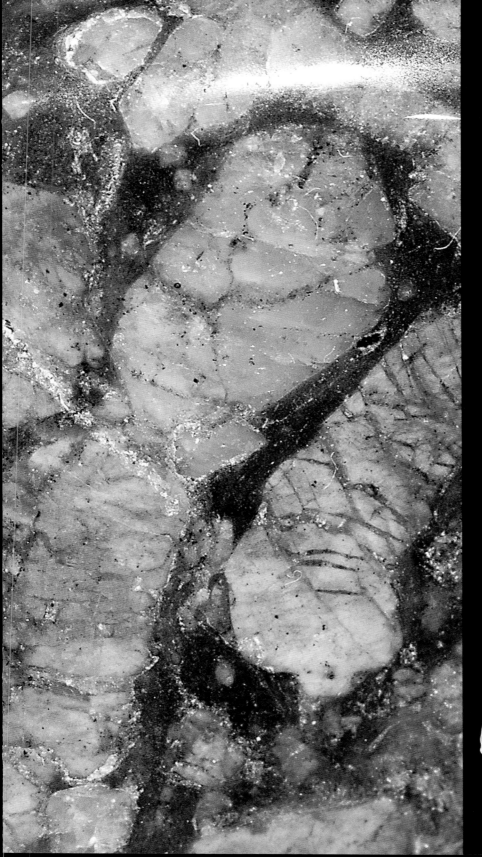

Alternative crystals

BLOODSTONE, AMBER

One of the oldest healing stones, Bloodstone has had more than five thousand years of use and has always been associated with strengthening the immune system and detoxifying the organs. It maintains the energetic purity of the blood, which in ancient times was regarded as the life force. Bloodstone was assigned magical properties and was believed to keep out the undesirable entities that caused disease. Amber has a similar healing history, drawing off toxins and stimulating the immune system to maintain optimum wellbeing.

BLOODSTONE

AMBER

QUARTZ, AMETRINE

Quartz is a master healing stone. Its internal matrix absorbs, amplifies and projects energy. Ametrine, with its mix of energizing Citrine and calming Amethyst, maintains optimum health. It is useful in chronic illness as it brings insight into the subtle causes of dis-ease.

AMETRINE

QUARTZ

QUE SERA IMMUNE-STIMULATOR PLACEMENT

How do I maintain optimum wellbeing?

This Que Sera healing placement infuses strong Qi into your immune system and stimulates the lymphatic system to drain toxins out of the body. Que Sera can also restore equilibrium to the chakras. You will need one or more Que Sera crystals, plus, ideally, a Clear Quartz and a Smoky Quartz stone.

1 Hold your Que Sera stone in your hand and connect to its power, feeling it radiating into your manifestation chakras and throughout your body.

2 To stimulate the immune system, lie down and place a Que Sera over your thymus gland (about a hand's breadth down from your throat).

3 If possible, place a Clear Quartz (point downward) in the centre of your forehead, and a Smoky Quartz (point down) at your feet.

4 Place your hands in your groin crease, one on each side, and lie still for ten minutes.

5 To rebalance the chakras, you either need a Que Sera for each chakra or to place a Que Sera on each chakra in turn for a minute or two, starting at your feet. If you are using one stone, cleanse it between chakras by rubbing a drop of crystal cleansing essence onto the stone.

CHAKRA IMBALANCES AND DIS-EASES

The chakras are linkage points between your aura and your physical body. Each chakra links to certain organs and conditions. Chakras below the waist tend to be primarily physical, although they can affect the endocrine glands and personality. Those in the upper torso are aligned to emotional functioning and psychosomatic conditions. Those in the head function on a mental and intuitive basis, but may have physical repercussions. Imbalance, blockage or disturbance of the chakras creates dis-ease, but the chakras can be restored to equilibrium using a healing crystal.

CHAKRA	DIS-EASES
Earth Star chakra (beneath the feet)	Dis-eases are lethargic: ME, arthritis, cancer, muscular disorders, depression, psychiatric disturbances, auto-immune diseases
Base chakra (base of the spine)	Dis-eases are constant, low-level or flare up suddenly: stiffness in the joints, chronic lower back pain, renal pain, fluid retention, reproductive or rectal disorders, constipation, diarrhea, varicose veins or hernias, bipolar disorder, glandular disturbances, personality and anxiety disorders, auto-immune diseases
Sacral chakra (below the navel)	Dis-eases are toxic and psychosomatic: PMT and muscle cramps, reproductive diseases, impotence, infertility, allergies, addictions, eating disorders, diabetes, liver or intestinal dysfunction, chronic back pain, urinary infections
Solar plexus chakra (above the waist)	Dis-eases are emotional and demanding: stomach ulcers, ME, 'fight or flight' adrenaline imbalances, insomnia, chronic anxiety, digestive problems, gallstones, pancreatic failure, skin conditions, eating disorders, phobias
Spleen chakra (below the left armpit)	Dis-eases arise from energetic and emotional depletion: lethargy, anemia, low blood sugar
Heart chakra (over the heart)	Dis-eases are psychosomatic and reactive: heart attacks, angina, chest infections, asthma, frozen shoulder, ulcers
Higher heart chakra (between the heart and throat)	Dis-eases follow the heart: arteriosclerosis, plus viral infections, tinnitus, epilepsy
Throat chakra (throat)	Dis-eases are active and block communication: sore throat/ quinsy, inflammation of the trachea, sinusitis, constant colds and viral infections, tinnitus, ear infections, jaw pain and gum disease, tooth problems, thyroid imbalances, high blood pressure, ADHD, autism, speech impediment, psychosomatic dis-eases
Third eye chakra (above and between the eyebrows)	Dis-eases are intuitive and metaphysical: migraines, mental overwhelm, schizophrenia, cataracts, iritis and other eye problems, epilepsy, autism, spinal and neurological disorders, sinus and ear infections, high blood pressure, 'irritations' of all kinds
Crown chakra (top of the head)	Dis-eases arise out of disconnection: metabolic syndrome, feeling 'unwell' with no known cause, nervous-system disturbances, electromagnetic and environmental sensitivity, depression, dementia, ME, insomnia or excessive sleepinesss, 'biological clock' disturbances such as jetlag
Past-life chakras (behind the ears)	Dis-eases include chronic illnesses, especially immune or endocrine deficiencies, genetic or physical malfunctions

Harmony and cooperation

Optimal manifestation is unselfish and is in harmony with the universe. Crystals teach us that, at a fundamental level, we are all one interconnected family, literally sharing the same essence. As John van Rees, the founder of Exquisite Crystals, said: 'When one person is in pain or suffers lack, we are all in pain.' I would add that, because of this interconnectedness, if even one crystal is misused to send harm to another soul, to 'come out on top' or bring benefit to someone to the detriment of others, then everyone (including the perpetrator) ultimately suffers. But if we bring more abundance, cooperation and peace into our lives, everyone benefits.

But where do we start? Well, as John van Rees also said, the place to generate peace is within our own self. From the personal to the collective – that is the answer. If we manifest peaceful harmony and cooperation inside ourselves, these qualities radiate out to the whole. We cannot change the world without changing ourselves. As we create our reality with every thought and action, peace and joyful abundance have to start from within. This is the butterflies not treacle approach: selfish ego-treacle mires us in the past, whereas serene butterflies fly free.

We're moving into the Age of Aquarius. This humanitarian sign of brotherhood asks how we create our future. It insists that we take personal responsibility for ourselves, our planet and all upon it. It points out that when one person shifts, the whole benefits. Under Aquarius – with a little adjustment, a tad more awareness and working together – we can put aside our individual egos and recognize ourselves as a soul-family with one aim: the evolution of consciousness in all its forms. Some courageous souls must go first, but, under Aquarius, they then turn around to give a hand to others.

We can step out of treacle and manifest with open-heartedness, honouring each soul's unique journey. We are butterflies dancing a new universe into being, polishing our souls to a brilliant shine. Just think how a million crystal butterflies beating their wings in unison could transform our world.

SPIRIT QUARTZ
Your harmony and cooperation crystal

Spirit Quartz synthesizes group efforts and brings about productive harmony. It is formed around a central core of Jasper or some other earthy stone. Tiny, high-vibration drusy Quartz crystals cover this core, reminding us that, at heart, we are all one and depend on one another. It also reminds us that the sum of the whole is greater than its constituent parts, and that more is achieved by cooperation than by competition.

UNDERSTANDING THIS CRYSTAL

Spirit Quartz grows as a group, even though it may appear as separate points. Multi-layered, one part depends on another, and no part exists without the support of the whole. It symbolizes the soul-group with which each soul travels, drawing sustenance and pulling the group together. High-vibration Spirit Quartz carries universal love and induces deep trance states, in which profound changes can be made to the way you perceive and create reality. With this crystal you traverse the multi-dimensions of consciousness to create harmony and joyful cooperation for the benefit of all.

The different colours of Spirit Quartz each help a different aspect of manifestation and heal the underlying causes of mis-manifestation. 'Amethyst' Spirit Quartz opens the higher crown chakra, aligning you to the infinity of being and bringing about the transmutation of prior misuses of power; setting you free from limitations, it encourages manifesting your highest spiritual potential. 'Citrine' Spirit Quartz assists feeling centred in your power and directing your life from your core. This stone purifies intent and is useful for accessing true abundance while releasing dependence on, or attachment to, material things; in business, it focuses goals and plans. 'Flame Aura' Spirit Quartz provides what each individual soul needs for its

spiritual evolution. 'Smoky' Spirit Quartz cleanses and releases deeply held emotions or states of dis-ease and traumatic memories, including those passed down the ancestral line to sabotage manifestation for later generations.

SPIRIT QUARTZ AND MANIFESTATION

Spirit Quartz assists in healing discord, and overcomes obsessive behaviour and deeply ingrained toxic patterns. Encouraging insightful dreams, it facilitates all metaphysical work, especially reframing the past. Bringing light into conflict and confusion, it creates a gentle, effective psychological and emotional detox that clears away the debris of the past, rejigging the etheric blueprint for the present life and healing cellular memory. It pinpoints significant karmic connections and highlights the gift of karmic justice in traumatic situations, promoting forgiveness for all.

USING SPIRIT QUARTZ

Meditating with Spirit Quartz provides insights into problems experienced within a community or a family, and can be activated to alleviate these and manifest harmony. Place it on an altar to bring about group cooperation and healing for the planet. Spirit Quartz also cleanses other stones and enhances their energy, when placed in a healing or abundance layout.

Alternative crystals

CANDLE QUARTZ, DRUSY AURORA QUARTZ, QUARTZ CLUSTER

Candle Quartz and Drusy Aurora Quartz (Anandalite™) instil tranquillity and assist in seeing beyond the confines of everyday circumstances to heal the ancestral line. Connecting to the divine love in your core being, they show when it is beneficial to share in a mutually supportive situation and when to stand alone. These crystals facilitate leaving – with loving grace – a relationship that no longer serves you. When placed in the centre of a group, they radiate unconditional love, creating group harmony. A Quartz Cluster works in the same way.

CANDLE QUARTZ

DRUSY AURORA QUARTZ

QUARTZ CLUSTER

CALCITE

Calcite has long been prized for its purity and its ability to bring about harmony in a group. Placing it in a room transmutes negative energies and calls in higher consciousness to facilitate group cooperation.

CALCITE

SPIRIT QUARTZ MEDITATION

How do I manifest harmony in my life and my community?

Harmony in your life and your community starts with peace in your own soul. If you have an unshakeable inner core of peace and serenity, then you cannot be swayed by external events and are always enfolded in harmony. You don't need to *do* anything in order to find peace or create harmony. Peace is who you are and what you radiate out to your community. It is a choice that you make, which no one can take away from you. Peace of mind is attainable no matter where you may be. And it generates yet more peace and harmony.

1 Hold your Spirit Quartz in your hand and connect to its power, feeling it radiating into your manifestation chakras (see page 30) and throughout your whole being.

2 With softly focused eyes, look carefully at your Spirit Quartz. Notice how tightly each tiny crystal fits against its neighbour and yet occupies its own space. Observe how the crystals cling around the central core to create a whole. Feel how each one supports the others, and yet remains an individual part of the whole.

3 Now close your eyes and concentrate on the peaceful feeling of the crystal radiating up your arms and down to your feet. Feel how your feet connect to the planet beneath you. Feel the stability that the Earth gives you: how it joins with the core of the crystal in a harmonious whole, giving strength and stability to your core being.

<u>4</u> Now concentrate on the peaceful feeling of the crystal radiating up your arms and into your heart. Store this peace in your heart. Place it at your core. Create a reservoir of peace and serenity on which to draw at each moment of the day or night.

<u>5</u> Let the peace radiate up into your head to settle into your mind. Let it calm your thoughts and harmonize them with your spiritual being. Know that you are one with the universe. Rest in this peace.

<u>6</u> Feel the wholeness of the crystal in your hands and how it resonates with the community around you. Let the peace radiate out from the crystal and from the manifestation chakras in your hands, so that it fills your immediate environment and then goes out to the wider world.

<u>7</u> With your left hand, place the crystal in a special place where it can continue to radiate peace out to the world. At the same time, touch your right hand to your forehead.

<u>8</u> Disconnect your attention, but retain your inner core of peaceful mind, body and spirit. Repeat the meditation at least once a day, even if it is only for a minute or two.

Attracting good fortune

If you put out generous good fortune to those around you, sharing what you have and being grateful for it, it draws abundance back to you. Attracting good fortune rests on the 'As above, so below; as below, so above' principle, which can also be translated as 'As you think, so you are'. Manifesting good fortune is supported by the powerful properties of prosperity-attuned crystals. Many of these crystals have been used for thousands of years and have thus been imbued with potent manifestation energy through belief and concentrated intention, which reinforces their powers in a self-supporting circle of beneficence.

Some people create their own luck, while others passively rely on outside fate or fortune. Some people are held back by awareness of their poverty and the belief that to be rich you must have money, while others know that – with good fortune on their side – there is always enough. When you recognize that abundance is an ongoing, universal flow with which you can harmonize, then you create your own good fortune. Gratitude comprises part of this flow: being thankful for what you have and counting your blessings increases them one-thousandfold. Make a point of saying thank you for everything you have, no matter how small the blessing might be. It is in the small things that your life is enriched. You will be amazed at how often the universe provides, even when you haven't made a request. Your good fortune increases exponentially, the more you pay attention to it. You will come to recognize that you have riches that are not connected with money. It is your inner resources, the friendships and experiences that you have and the value that you put on them that make you truly rich.

However, you can harness the manifesting forces that emanate throughout the universe, drawing them down to support and expand your manifestation. This is where a combination of attraction-triangles and your chakras come in. Integrate the two and you can empower your whole subtle-energy system (a biomagnetic energy capsule that works in harmony with the physical and psychic bodies to mediate energy flow), magnetizing it to attract good fortune on all levels.

JADE
Your good-fortune crystal

Jade is a stone of good fortune, long used to attract abundance of all kinds. It helps you to be grateful for what you already have. Ancient New Zealand lore says that, when given and received with love, Jade takes on the spirit of those who wear it and acts as a link between giver and receiver. Passed down through a family, it carries the spirit of the ancestors.

UNDERSTANDING THIS CRYSTAL

A stone of good luck that supports taking a gamble, Jade helps you reconnect to the universal flow and to karmic gifts developed over many lifetimes. Meditate with it to find your true talents. It helps you see the real value of money and your own worth, so that you realize that all you need lies within you. A profoundly spiritual stone, Jade encourages you to recognize that, as a spiritual being, you have access to much wider powers and multi-dimensions. It encourages you to become all that you can be.

JADE AND MANIFESTATION

If you have issues around money (whether from lack, over-extravagance or worshipping this false god), Jade will assist you in overcoming them. This serene crystal reminds you to nurture your talents and maximize your potential, drawing on the wisdom of the ancestors and on skills handed down through the family. Encouraging self-sufficiency, it symbolizes the purity of intention that is required for clear manifestation. It also helps you to think laterally and find creative solutions to problems. At the same time it draws to you people with integrity and insight.

Jade integrates your personality with your inner resources, reminding you that 'God helps those who help themselves.' It helps you to break down complex ideas so that they become less daunting to put into practice. Jade is protective and assists you in conserving and making the most of what you have, even when this seems very little.

USING JADE

The Chinese believe that Jade transfers its virtues into your body and purifies your energies. When placed on the soma chakra (midway along your hairline) or under your pillow, Jade promotes insightful dreams and helps you to dream something new into being. Use it to understand how best to manifest what you are seeking and to recognize what may have been blocking your efforts. It also releases negative core beliefs. Wear Jade or keep it in your cashbox to invite prosperity into your life.

Red Jade, the most stimulating kind, helps you to turn anger into energy that empowers your manifesting. Use Blue-Green Jade to make steady progress in manifesting your goals; it assists if you feel overwhelmed by circumstances beyond your control. Brown Jade earths your energies and helps you adapt to your environment, while Lavender Jade assists you in establishing clear boundaries and holds back emotional excess. Mellow Yellow Jade teaches the interconnectedness of all things. White Jade helps you access all relevant information when assessing situations. Maori Greenstone Jade is a master healer and powerful manifestor.

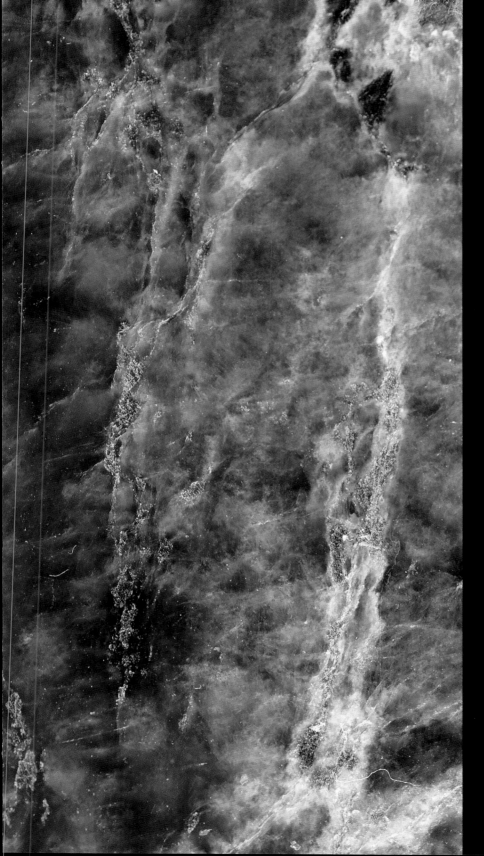

Alternative crystals

GOLDSTONE, AVENTURINE, CITRINE

Alchemically created Goldstone is often known as 'the money stone' and is used to manifest good fortune of every kind. Aventurine, which resembles Goldstone, and Citrine have also long enjoyed a reputation as powerful manifestors of abundance. They draw the energizing strength of the sun down to the Earth to power manifestation and attract prosperity.

GOLDSTONE

CITRINE

AVENTURINE

TIGER'S EYE

Long used as a talisman against curses and ill-luck, Tiger's Eye helps to harmonize the positive and negative forces in the universe, supporting necessary change. It strengthens your will, teaches the right use of power and helps you to clarify your intention so that you manifest at the highest level.

TIGER'S EYE

JADE LAYOUT
How do I manifest good fortune?

Jade has always attracted good fortune, and this layout combines the powerful manifesting properties of triangles and chakras with this abundant stone. The overlapping triangles create an 'as above, so below' multi-dimensional grid, which harnesses the universal energy of good fortune contained in Jade and the universe, so that abundance manifests on Earth. Although you can do this grid alone, a helper makes laying out the crystals easier and allows you to focus your intention quietly on what you are seeking to manifest. A helper can also join up the triangles as you create them, using a Jade or Quartz wand.

1 Hold 2 large pieces of jade and 11 tumbled stones in your hand and connect to their power, feeling it radiating into your manifestation chakras and throughout your whole being.

2 State your intention clearly and then lie down in a comfortable position.

3 Place a large piece of Jade facing downward about 30 cm (12 in) beneath your feet and another one facing downward above your head.

4 Open each manifestation chakra (see page 30). Place your hands down at your side, with the palms facing in and your hands about 30 cm (12 in) from your body.

5 Open your base and sacral chakras by picturing them unfolding like flower petals. With your mind, form a triangle between your palms and up to the Dantien, which sits above your sacral chakra. This triangle encompasses the base and sacral chakras. Place a tumbled Jade on each point and, if you have a helper, ask them to join up the triangle, or use your mind to do so.

6 Open your solar-plexus, heart and throat chakras. From the top of your sacral chakra (just below the Dantien), draw the base of a triangle with your mind and take the apex up to the heart (see diagram). Place a tumbled Jade on each point of the triangle.

7 Make another, intersecting triangle from the solar plexus to the brow chakra, which opens. Place a tumbled Jade on each point of this triangle. Ask your helper to link the points with a wand, or do so with your mind. The triangles encompass and link your solar plexus, heart and throat chakras.

8 Visualize whatever you wish to bring into manifestation. Feel the energy in your palms as it moves through the triangles and up to your third eye.

9 From the Jade above your head create an upside-down triangle, which reaches out to the sides and down to a point about 30 cm (12 in) below your feet, activating the Earth Star chakra on which the large Jade sits. Opening this chakra anchors your intention and manifestation in the Earth.

10 Feel how it is when your manifestation is complete.

11 Now take your attention away, remove the stones and let the triangles do their work.

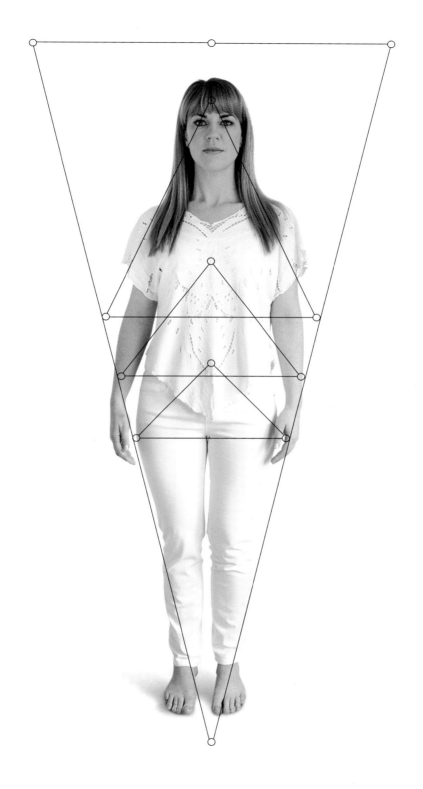

Keeping your energy high

If your physical, mental and spiritual energies are not functioning at their optimum, then your manifesting cannot work. If your mental energy is low, you will lack ideas or motivation. If your physical energy is low, you will lack the ability to put ideas into practice and actually manifest them in everyday reality; your dreams remain precisely that – dreams. If your spiritual energy is low, you will manifest for selfish reasons in a spirit of combative competition, which is unlikely to result in success. But if all those energies are in balance and you have a reservoir of fuel in the Dantien (the body's creative energy storehouse), you manifest with ease.

Physical energy is stored in the Dantien but is depleted by excessive stress or by trying too hard with your manifestation. If you put in huge amounts of effort, it is counterproductive. Focusing your intention and trusting the universe is more productive. The Dantien is the body's centre of gravity as well as its energy store for Qi, or life force. A constantly revolving sphere, it sits on top of the sacral chakra and acts as a kind of higher octave of that chakra, to refine and stimulate creativity and fertilize new ideas. If you are to be dynamic and empowered, this storehouse needs replenishing. Fortunately, a simple activation accomplishes this and is greatly strengthened by the addition of a high-energy crystal.

To keep your mental energy high, your mind needs to be stimulated and active, but not overactive. If you are too busy to hear the suggestions that your inner guidance is offering, manifesting becomes futile. Depression must be kept at bay, and dreaming (though creative) must be held at an appropriate level and converted into action. Remember that what the mind can conceive, it can achieve, but it needs the space to do this, so switch it off by meditating on a regular basis. Mental energy is wasted in thoughts such as 'What if I had…?' or 'If only I could…' and they need to be banished if you are to succeed in your manifesting.

CARNELIAN
Your crystal energizer

A favourite healing stone of the ancient Egyptians, who used it to maintain the vitality of young children and give them protection, Carnelian is an excellent crystal for energizing any part of your life. It kick-starts the manifesting process, activates your creativity and gives you the physical and mental energy to move forward. It also has the ability to cleanse and re-energize other stones.

UNDERSTANDING THIS CRYSTAL

Carnelian grounds and anchors your manifesting in the present reality. If you're a daydreamer rather than a doer, it helps to make things happen in everyday reality. A stabilizing stone, it is excellent for restoring vitality and motivation and for stimulating creativity. One of Carnelian's greatest gifts is that of providing powerful protection against envy, rage and resentment. If other people's jealousy is blocking your progress, Carnelian releases this. It also helps to instil love and trust after abuse of any kind, restoring confidence. If you have suffered from resentment yourself, it calms anger and banishes emotional negativity, replacing it with a love of life that empowers you to manifest your dreams.

CARNELIAN AND MANIFESTATION

Carnelian is filled with life force and vitality, which dispel apathy and motivate you toward success in business and other matters. At a physical level, it energetically improves the absorption of vitamins and minerals, and ensures a good supply of blood to your organs, muscles and tissues – necessary for efficient functioning. Stimulating the metabolism, this invigorating stone gets you into optimum physical condition for manifesting. At a more subtle level, it activates the base and sacral chakras, freeing up blockages, and raises the Kundalini energy of creativity, increasing fertility on all levels. If you have been feeling impotent, this stone restores potency and makes things happen.

Carnelian lifts depression, especially in those of more advanced years. At a psychological level, this crystal imparts awareness and acceptance of the cycle of life. In ancient times it protected the dead on their journey, and so it removes the fear of death that can paralyse risk-taking. This stone helps you trust yourself and your perceptions. Imparting enormous courage, it assists in making positive life choices. Meditate with it to get to the bottom of what makes you tick. With its assistance you can overcome negative conditioning and find steadfastness of purpose. At a mental level, Carnelian helps manifestation by improving your analytic abilities and clarifying your perception so that you become more focused. It sharpens concentration, dispels mental lethargy and blocks out extraneous thought in meditation.

USING CARNELIAN

Traditionally Carnelian is worn as a pendant, bracelet or belt buckle. Alternatively, keep it in your pocket to maintain your energy levels. Red Carnelian combats sluggishness and invigorates your mind and body. A Carnelian near the front door provides protection and invites abundance into your home.

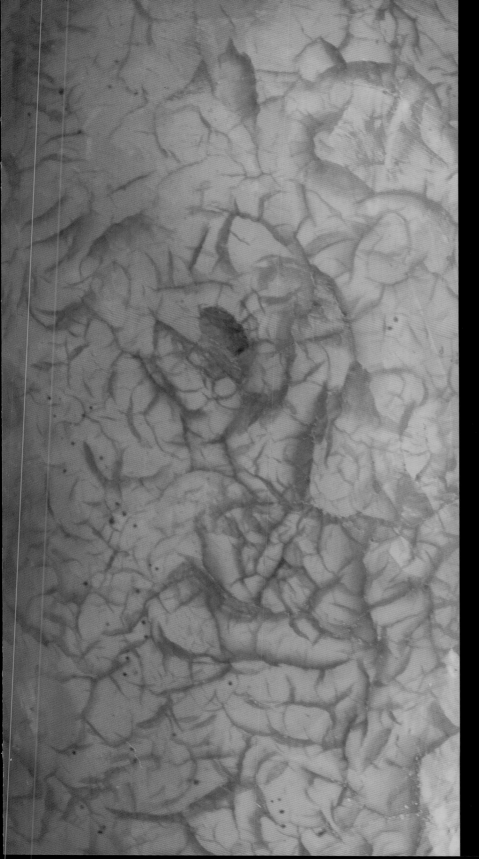

Alternative crystals

RED JASPER, POPPY JASPER

Red Jasper has long been credited with the power to energize and get things moving; it stimulates the lust for life. Poppy Jasper moves things on quickly or gently, as appropriate, and provides new motivation, encouraging cooperation rather than competition. This stone helps recognize the value of right timing, and holds back precipitate action. If your base chakra is overactive, Poppy Jasper calms it.

RED JASPER

POPPY JASPER

QUE SERA, FIRE AGATE

Que Sera is an excellent stone when you need more energy, for it positively fizzes; it will spice up any area of your life. Protective Fire Agate, on the other hand, calms and grounds your energy into the base chakra, so that ideas manifest in the physical world.

QUE SERA

FIRE AGATE

CARNELIAN ENERGY JUMP-START

How do I get myself moving?

Feeling fully alive and totally energized is essential for the manifesting process. This is what keeps you going, helping you to help yourself at each moment of the day. This activation is particularly beneficial first thing in the morning, especially if you are a sluggish person who finds the mornings a challenge, as it helps you leap out of bed and start the manifesting process immediately, giving you the energy to function. But it is also a useful pick-me-up if your energy flags at any time during the day. Use it whenever you need extra motivation or the energy to complete a task.

1 Stand with your feet slightly apart and your knees bent a little, feet flat on the floor. Let your arms hang loosely, with your hands cupped one on top of the other just below your navel – experiment to find which hand feels more comfortable on top. Hold a cleansed Carnelian gently in your cupped palms. Connect to its power, feeling it radiating into your manifestation chakras and throughout your whole being. Focus your attention on the Carnelian in your hands until you feel it begin to heat up and glow.

2 Now focus on the area of your belly immediately behind your hands. This is the Dantien, the energy centre that sits just below the navel and above the sacral chakra. It is a power store for your physical body.

3 With each in-breath, draw energy in through the crystal and into the Dantien. Allow the energy to collect there until the Dantien fizzes and feels fully energized.

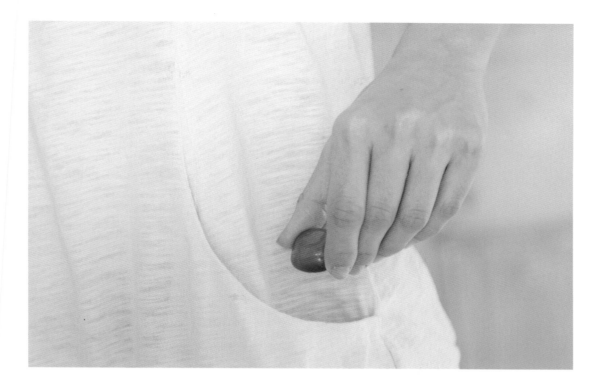

4 When the Dantien is fully charged, breathe in and let the energy rush up your body and into your mind and then, as you breathe out, spread out into all levels of your being.

5 If you feel at all 'floaty' or light-headed, take your attention down to your feet and imagine that you have an anchor connecting you to the centre of the Earth.

6 Do this activation for five minutes, pulling energy in from the Carnelian whenever the Dantien begins to feel depleted, and ensuring that you finish with your Dantien fully energized to give you abundant energy for the day.

7 Pop the Carnelian in your pocket and hold it whenever you need a quick boost.

Making decisions

Are you a chronic ditherer veering between two points of view, unable to make up your mind or too afraid to step into the unknown? Or do you rush headlong into decisions, only to regret them later? Neither of these stances is helpful when manifesting. People who manifest effectively are also good decision-makers. They know what they want, formulate how to get there and go for it. Clear, considered decisions make the manifesting process flow much more smoothly, as there are no underlying conflicts or procrastination to get in the way.

There are many factors that can unconsciously affect your decision-making. Previous experience, emotional baggage, false beliefs, frustration and fear of what other people may think (or an attempt to please them) can sabotage your manifesting. Many decisions will take you outside your comfort zone, so you may tend unconsciously to resort to the default setting – 'the known' – no matter how stultifying that may be. Constant worry, or a tendency to think inside the box, also halts the decision-making process. Creative solutions arise when you step out of the known and into unknown territory, which is why your intuition and your subconscious mind can be great allies. These are steps to a productive decision:

- Identify your main objective or goal and focus on it. Do not get sidetracked.
- Recognize any underlying fears or conflicts that you may have. Be tolerant but firm with yourself; be aware of their effect and then put them to one side.
- Mobilize your rational mind, your organizational and analytical skills to assess the data and set out the choices or possibilities with clarity.
- Hand the process over to your intuition to provide the answer.
- Once you've reached a decision, take action. Avoid procrastination and delaying tactics. Go for it!

Research has shown that even a few minutes of meditation each day greatly enhance the decision-making process, and that dream-incubation is a time-honoured way of turning problems into opportunities.

OWYHEE BLUE OPAL
Your decision crystal

With its celestial vibration, Owyhee Blue Opal connects you to the highest of guidance and assists in incubating insightful dreams. This stone opens your metaphysical abilities, heightening intuition and facilitating kything – two-way communication with the spirit world. Helping you to be more courageous in your decision-making, it strengthens your personal power and your ability to manifest a new reality.

UNDERSTANDING THIS CRYSTAL

A stone of actualization, Owyhee Blue Opal is formed from microscopic silica spheres, which bond to water inside the stone to create a luminescent glow. Discovered in 2003 near a sacred Indian spring, this Opal is unique. Its intense colour reflects the serenity of a summer sky, calming the soul, softening stress and instilling mental peacefulness, no matter what the future holds.

Owyhee Blue Opal forms a powerful connection between your third eye and soma chakras, helping you to be in incarnation and to travel through the multi-dimensions of consciousness. It stimulates your inner sight and the ability to perceive the subtle world. Expanding your awareness and enhancing your power of perception, with this stone you pick up the subtle clues and signals that point the way forward and enlighten your decisions.

This stone has traditionally been used to facilitate shamanic journeying and to explore different timeframes. It assists your communication with all higher beings and facilitates verbalizing your own insights and holding fast to the truth. Used to invoke lucid dreaming, Owyhee Blue Opal can also help you dream a new world into being.

OWYHEE BLUE OPAL AND MANIFESTATION

Owyhee Blue Opal balances the mind and the emotions. It helps you to be more confident and outgoing, dispelling shyness and anxiety and overcoming fear of failure. Facilitating healing the wounds of the past, it helps you to reach with ease the goals you set for yourself. This stone activates and draws on your personal power, but assists you to manifest it without becoming bombastic or arrogant in the process. This is an excellent stone for personal development, expansion and forward progress. It synthesizes your powers of perception, self-expression and the will to motivate your life. Releasing feelings of powerlessness, it enables you to choose which action (or non-action) is the best means of achieving your goals.

USING OWYHEE BLUE OPAL

If you suffer from indecision or mental confusion, place this Opal on your forehead between your third eye and soma chakra, or on the back of the skull, to clear negative mental patterns and expectations. This luminous stone instils clarity and assists in finding exactly the right words for a given situation. Use it to give you confidence and clarity when speaking in public or formulating your intention.

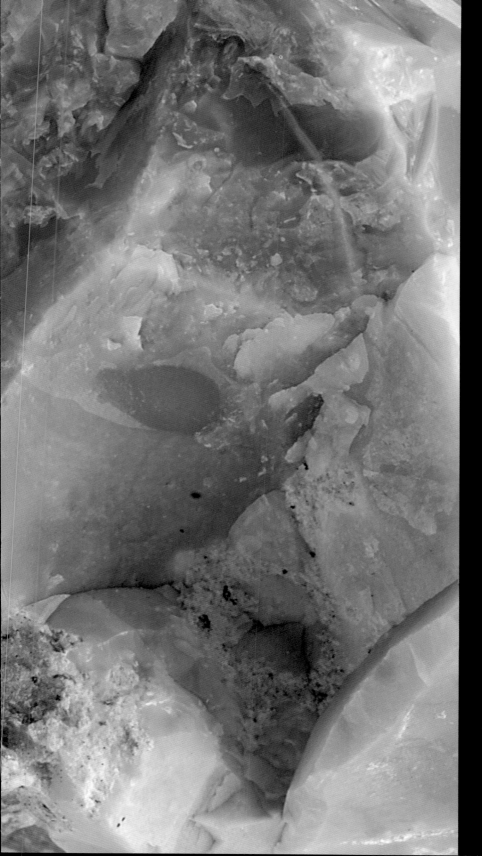

Alternative crystals

DIASPORE (ZULTANITE), STONE OF DREAMS™

If you seem incapable of living out your dream, Diaspore will pinpoint the changes needed to manifest action. This stone gives you the courage to break free from limiting patterns and to bounce back even after enormous setbacks, as does the Stone of Dreams. If you have plans that you never fulfil, or aspirations that always seem out of reach, these stones bring fruition. Opening and clarifying your mind, you will find inspiration that enables you to think outside the box.

STONE OF DREAMS™

DIASPORE

ANDALUSITE™, DREAM QUARTZ

Andalusite attracts bizarre or dreamlike situations that assist in understanding the deeper meaning of your life; to an open mind, it reveals hidden wisdom. Dream Quartz promotes insightful lucid dreams and dream recall, and supports dreaming up a new future.

ANDALUSITE™

DREAM QUARTZ

OWYHEE BLUE OPAL DREAMING

How do I find an answer?

In the temples of old, dream chambers allowed querents (enquirers) to incubate a dream that answered their most pressing question. You can create a dream temple in your own home and use the same tools to manifest an answer. If you become aware that you are dreaming, you can influence the course of the dream: lucid dreaming allows you to try out various scenarios, or takes you to meet a council of wise ones who hold the answers. Dreams also give you clues from the past, and in a lucid dream you can go back in time to reconnect to skills that will assist you in the present lifetime.

1 Choose a night when you can take time the following morning to process the dream. Abstain from alcohol, drugs, caffeine and nicotine for a couple of hours before bedtime. Take a long, leisurely bath to which you have added rose or clary-sage oil (do not use if you are pregnant), which encourages dreaming.

2 Burn relaxing candles and gaze into your crystal. Hold your stone in your hand and connect to its power, feeling it radiating into your manifestation chakras and throughout your whole being. Activate it so that when you place it under your pillow, it helps you dream true and wisely.

3 Before going to bed, sip hot chocolate spiced with nutmeg and cinnamon. Dress in clean night attire. Place a small pillow on top of your usual pillows, so that you are sleeping higher than usual and on your right side. Place your crystal under this pillow, or hold it in your hand.

4 As you go to sleep, picture yourself entering an ancient dream temple, lying down on one of the specially prepared beds and getting ready to put your question to the wise ones. Contemplate the issue on which you need dream guidance. Look at the solutions you have already tried and the actions you have taken. Ask yourself whether you are ready to manifest your desires. If there are emotional issues, are you prepared to let go? Do you need to change any beliefs about yourself? State your question clearly. Tell yourself that, when you awake, you will remember the dream answer. Look as far to the left as possible without turning your head, and then to the right.

5 Put the question aside and sleep. If you become aware that you are dreaming, ask to be shown the possible outcomes so that you can explore for yourself the manifestation that would be appropriate, or go into the past to gain further insight.

6 As soon as you wake up, record your dream.

Stimulating your creativity

Being in the creative flow means being fully present in the now and completely immersed in the creative process from moment to moment, looking neither backward nor forward. Fear of failure is one of the major factors that hinder creativity. Rather than viewing previous manifestation attempts negatively, perceiving your failures as learning experiences helps you to refine the way you approach the process. Although failure may not seem productive, neither is doing nothing, so don't allow yourself to be caught in the inactivity trap. Encourage yourself to take risks, to do the unexpected, the bizarre and the surprising. Often the best ideas arise out of playfulness and humour. Don't worry about the future or how to bring these creative ideas into manifestation. Simply have them – and believe that there is a creative outcome.

If you are to manifest creatively, you need to change your mindset. Challenge your old assumptions. Think laterally, and suddenly the future will look brighter. Always believe that everything has a solution. If you are optimistic, you'll soon find that you begin to think outside the box. You will work around the solution, no matter how bizarre it may seem at first glance. You can also work backward, from having the result to how you'll achieve it. Redefine the 'problem' or the goal – reword it. Stand it on its head or come at it from a completely different angle. Often the very act of putting the 'problem' another way turns it into a challenge and opens up new possibilities.

Using a different mode of recording your goal also works wonders. The act of cutting, arranging and pasting pictures on a vision board, for instance, takes you out of your analytical, logical brain and into your receptive, intuitive faculties and involves your body in the process. The seemingly random pattern that you make may show you a surprising answer – and leave room for serendipitous synchronicity to take its place in your life. Stepping back and looking at the vision board helps you to shift to a more objective perspective, but if you've included the unexpected, it might also surprise you with a solution.

GARNET
Your creativity crystal

Innovative Garnet stimulates light-bulb moments and helps you think outside the box. It motivates you to be more creative in your life and to do the unexpected, empowering your manifesting abilities. One of the most plentiful stones, Garnet takes on different forms and colours, each of which has specific properties in addition to its generic attributes, but red and orange are the strongest creativity stimulators.

UNDERSTANDING THIS CRYSTAL

Garnet is an energizing and regenerative stone, especially for the base and sacral chakras, although it also works on the heart. It revitalizes, purifies and balances energy in these chakras, bringing serenity or passion as appropriate. Assisting in letting go of outworn ideas, this is a useful stone for dissolving emotional blockages and sharpening your innate perception. Dissolving ingrained behaviour patterns that no longer serve you, it helps bypass resistance or unconscious sabotage. This crystal also removes inhibitions and taboos, facilitating thinking and doing the previously unthinkable.

If your sacral chakra (located just below your navel) is blocked or out of balance, then experiencing yourself as a powerful, sexual, potent being is impossible. Clean up that chakra and you will feel confident, with high self-esteem, and your creativity will flow. Placing Garnet on the base and sacral chakras helps you to overcome fear of failure. These chakras are where your survival instinct lies, as well as your courage and fortitude, and Garnet stimulates these qualities, turning a crisis into an opportunity. The sacral chakra can also hold 'hooks' from people with whom you have had a sexual relationship, which can stop the flow of creative energy. Garnet helps to dissolve these hooks and re-energize the chakras so that you become self-empowered.

Dynamic and flexible, Brown Andraite Garnet attracts into your relationships whatever you most need for your development. It dissolves feelings of isolation or alienation. Orangey-red Hessonite Garnet eliminates guilt and inferiority and encourages you to seek out new challenges, while blood-red Pyrope Garnet bestows vitality and charisma.

GARNET AND MANIFESTATION

If you have been feeling impotent, or are stuck in plans that have not manifested, Garnet helps you to move out of the feelings of 'stuckness' into potent action. It is an extremely useful crystal in situations where there seems to be no way out, or where life has become fragmented or traumatic. Garnet offers hope in apparently hopeless situations. It also promotes mutual assistance in times of trouble.

USING GARNET

A powerful attractor of abundance, hexagonal green or red Grossular Garnet is an effective stone for creating a pentangle or a Star of David layout. It draws prosperity into your life and gives support during challenges, helping you to go with the flow and manifesting cooperation and friendship. Wearing a square-cut Garnet traditionally ensures success in business dealings.

Alternative crystals

RUBY, BLOOD OF ISIS, CARNELIAN

Like Garnet, Ruby is a powerful energizer for the base chakra and this, especially when combined with Carnelian on the sacral chakra, helps the creative force to rise, activating your manifesting power. The rare red Blood of Isis – gem-quality Carnelian that was popular in ancient Egypt – makes a very powerful connection to the creative energies of the Mother Goddess and helps you to remember lost parts of yourself.

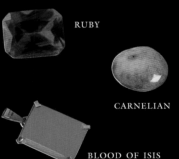

RUBY

CARNELIAN

BLOOD OF ISIS

TANGERINE QUARTZ

Vibrant Tangerine Quartz is coloured by iron, as are other yellow and orange Quartzes. All stimulate new ideas and different ways of approaching old problems. This energetic stone helps you to move out of stuck situations and into fresh activity.

TANGERINE QUARTZ

ACTIVATING YOUR CREATIVITY
The vision board

Once your base and sacral chakras are cleansed and energized, making a vision board gets your creativity moving. It enables you to put as many wild and wacky ideas as possible out to the universe, knowing that this triggers a creative flow. On your vision board put images of all that you desire, no matter how far out of reach it may seem. Don't let low self-esteem or thoughts of 'I don't deserve this' or a lack of confidence hamper you. Be as outrageous as possible. The idea is to show yourself, and the universe, that you have a vision of a different, vibrant, potent self. You will need a selection of Garnets (one Red, one Orange and five Grossular Garnets), a collection of images, glue and a piece of cardboard.

1 Hold your stones in your hand and connect to their power, feeling it radiating into your manifestation chakras and throughout your whole being.

2 Place a cleansed and charged Red Garnet on your base chakra and an Orange Garnet on your sacral chakra. Lie still for 15 minutes and absorb the energy, so that you are fully empowered and your chakras fizz with energy. Then remove the stones and put them to one side.

3 Collect together as many pictures as possible of everything that you would like to see in your life – no matter how ridiculous, outrageous, bizarre and downright laughable you think they may seem. Be playful and humorous in your choices. Cultivate optimism as you do this, and suspend judgment as to whether it is practical or sensible.

4 Stick the pictures onto a large piece of cardboard, overlapping them so that there are no gaps in the energy. Put images of confident, creative people on the board, as well as items, places, situations and gifts that you seek to manifest in your life.

5 When the board is complete, lie it down and, with your left hand, place five large Grossular Garnets in a pentangle shape (see page 27). Join up the lines by tracing the shape with your fingers.

6 Touch your forehead with the stones that you placed on your chakras and then put them in the centre of the board, the Orange Garnet above the Red Garnet.

7 If possible, stick these stones in place and display the board on your wall so that you see it often.

Healing mind, body and soul

True healing comes from inner wholeness – a fusion of body, mind and soul – and from congruence with your soul and its multi-dimensional intentions. Congruence means that all levels are in a state of harmonious equilibrium and that wellbeing flows. D.H. Lawrence said, 'I am ill because of wounds to the soul, to the deep emotional self.' Dis-ease is subtle and does not always manifest as physical illness. It occurs on emotional, mental and spiritual levels, and is carried through the karmic or ancestral line. Soul-dis-ease arises out of wounds, attitudes, contracts and patterns carried forward from the past into the present via the 'etheric blueprint' – the subtle-energy grid that creates the new physical body. 'Dis-ease' may also offer an opportunity to develop attributes such as patience, tolerance and compassion, or may give someone else a chance to grow. Karma is not a matter of blame, but one of balancing out the past so that a soul evolves. Healing does not necessarily mean 'getting better'. If health is not restored, it may be from soul-choice, or the soul may not have finished evolving through that condition. The soul may be trying to 'get better' for the wrong reasons or may be entrenched in 'reparation-restitution'. A soul leaves incarnation when it has learned all it needs so that it can incarnate again and put the lessons into practice. But, while the soul is here, the inner state can be one of wellbeing and quiet joy.

Karmic or ancestral causes of dis-ease include:
- Soul-unrest
- The intention to develop specific qualities
- Past-life repression of pain refusing to be ignored
- Remaining on the karmic treadmill
- Attitudinal karma: old attitudes manifested as a physical condition
- Bigotry or lack of empathy for others
- Organic karma: carrying over affliction or disability
- Symbolic karma: dis-ease mimicking the cause
- Redemptive karma: helping someone else
- Conflict from several past-life personas
- A strongly negative past-life self manifesting again
- Past-life vows and promises holding the soul back

AMPHIBOLE
Your master healing crystal

Joyful Amphibole is known as 'Angel Phantom' because of the inner wings it displays and the ethereal angelic vibration that it carries. This crystal connects to the highest levels of spiritual experience, helping you to become one with the cosmos and unite that with our world. It takes you into a place pulsating with energy and *knowing*. This unity consciousness promotes profound soul and psychic healing.

UNDERSTANDING THIS CRYSTAL

A form of Quartz, Amphibole is a fusion of several minerals and so represents unity of the whole. Within the energizing clear-Quartz coating, its phantoms and inclusions (the pyramid shapes, small crystals or mineral fragments and bubbles within the crystal point) incorporate red Hematite, a deeply stable stone that offers protection, grounds your energies and dissolves negativity; white Kaolinite, which opens the inner ear so that you hear the voice of your spiritual guides; and yellow-peach Limonite, which guards against psychic attack or mental influence. Phantoms symbolize the numerous lifetimes of the soul and take you travelling through the multi-dimensions of reality. They break up old patterns and assist in reconnecting to the ancient wisdom held in your soul-memory.

Amphibole helps you call in your guardian angel. Its gentle and calming energy releases worry and trauma and activates a deep inner joy. With this stone you are always centred in the present moment. It is helpful for letting go of the past and for dissolving the psychosomatic causes of dis-ease.

AMPHIBOLE AND MANIFESTATION

Gazing into Amphibole's depths takes you into a space of deep universal love and assists you in acting from a place of love. Its phantoms and inclusions help you to manifest from a coherent, congruent place within yourself that is in harmony with the universe. This crystal facilitates manifestation that is for the good of the whole, especially that which assists your spiritual evolution and the expansion of your consciousness. Amphibole's protective function and its connection to higher dimensions also make the stone a useful companion for spiritual journeying and visualizations.

USING AMPHIBOLE

Placing Amphibole on the crown chakra activates all the higher crown chakras above your head, opening up a ladder that awareness can ascend to connect with your soul and the highest guidance. Placing Amphibole over the third eye facilitates introspection and insight, as it attunes you to the wisdom of the universal mind. It helps you to take a more detached perspective on life and on your spiritual evolution. If you need to know why your manifestation is, seemingly, not working or is operating in a different way from how you had envisaged, meditating with this stone reveals the deeper causes and soul-intention. Triangulating three Amphiboles creates a perfect meditation or creative space. In the workplace, this crystal subtly shifts your energies to the highest level possible and facilitates cooperation and harmony. Keep Amphibole in your pocket for continuous healing.

Alternative crystals

QUANTUM QUATTRO

Combining Shattuckite,
Dioptase, Malachite and
Chrysocolla in Smoky Quartz,
Quantum Quattro heals grief,
releases heartache, draws out toxic
emotions and psychosomatic
causes, breaks unwanted ties and
outworn patterns, and teaches you
how to take responsibility for your
actions, thoughts and feelings.
It assists in recognizing your
resources and helps indicate
direction. It has a dramatic effect
on the human energy field.
Grounding spiritual energies,
it also brings about a better world.
Visualize positive changes with it,
to offset negative expectations.

QUANTUM
QUATTRO

GOLDEN HEALER
QUARTZ

With concentrated universal life
force, Golden Healer Quartz
potentizes healing on all levels. A
catalyst for expanded consciousness
it harnesses the personal will to the
divine, so that soul – rather than
ego – becomes the guiding light.
This stone facilitates manifesting
profound changes with the
minimum of effort.

GOLDEN HEALER QUARTZ

AMPHIBOLE VISUALIZATION
How do I heal multi-dimensionally?

This Amphibole visualization is a potent way to release all the issues that lie behind dis-ease (physical or psychic), especially the psychosomatic and karmic layers. It facilitates stepping into multi-dimensional soul-healing so that you manifest from a whole, healed, high-vibrational perspective. It is truly holistic, working on the body, emotions, mind and soul to purify and bring them into alignment. It calls in angelic helpers to assist with your manifestation and to ensure that you feel totally safe and supported within your world. Before entering the fountain of healing, turn off your mobile phone and ensure that you are not disturbed for 10–15 minutes.

1 Hold your stone in your hand and connect to its power, feeling it radiating into your manifestation chakras and throughout your whole being. Then set up the Amphibole point in a cleansed and dedicated sacred space (an altar is ideal).

2 Sit with the Amphibole in front of you at eye level, if possible, or slightly below. Breathe gently and easily, establishing a comfortable rhythm. With your eyes half-closed, look up to a point slightly above and between your eyebrows, then gaze at the crystal until your eyes go out of focus.

3 Picture a fountain of light pulsing up from the base of the crystal and flowing out in a beautiful rainbow of colour. Immerse yourself in this healing light. Feel it infusing every level of your being, releasing tension and blockages and bringing you into equilibrium and harmony. Rest in this peace for as long as you wish, feeling it penetrate each and every cell in your body.

4 When you are ready, breathe deeply, open your eyes and disengage your attention from the crystal. Stand up and feel the contact that your feet make with the floor.

5 Carrying a tumbled Amphibole in your pocket means that you are continuously bathed in its healing energy.

Finding love

If you want to find love, you must become a magnet for love by radiating love out to the world, and you must be ready to receive it equally in return. So, think carefully. Is your love imbalanced: do you always give more than you receive, or are you trying to force love to come to you? Manifesting love does not involve trying to make someone else love you. You manifest love because you are loving, not because you demand it. If you manifest the 'same old, same old', you may need to think about changing your pattern. Unconditional love is the most constructive basis for all relationships. But unconditional love needs to be extended to yourself as well as others. If you do not love yourself, how can anyone else love you? Unconditional love sets boundaries, but for yourself, not the other person. It does not get entangled in someone's dramas, nor does it force changes because you can see how wonderful they could be – that is manipulation. Unconditional love offers loving acceptance whilst someone else sorts out their own life. It means saying, 'I love you, and at the same time I am taking care of myself by staying in a good space within myself.' It certainly does not mean abuse, victimization or domination. There are times when the most loving thing you can do for someone – and for yourself – is to walk away.

A crystal, infused with positive regard and unconditional love, never judges you or puts you down. With its assistance you can enjoy an abundance of love. Crystals encourage you to love fully. They facilitate forgiveness – essential if you are to be truly free to love. Forgiving, and accepting forgiveness, are signs of emotional maturity. You may need to forgive people from your past or present, or accept forgiveness from others, to cleanse your manifestation of its old patterns. Saying the forgiveness affirmation below, every time you feel angry or challenged, is a great way to keep emotionally healthy and fully loving – and to manifest a loving relationship for yourself:

> *I forgive anyone who has wronged me in any timeframe, and I accept forgiveness from anyone I have wronged. I profoundly and deeply love, accept and forgive myself.*

ROSE QUARTZ
Your love crystal

Nothing manifests love better than a beautiful piece of Rose Quartz.
The empathetic energies of Rose Quartz help you to love unconditionally
and to forgive yourself and other people. This stone of acceptance teaches
the essence of true love and instils infinite peace into your heart.
Releasing emotional wounds, it heals and opens your heart on every level.

UNDERSTANDING THIS CRYSTAL

Rose Quartz is the finest heart-healer. Releasing
unexpressed emotions and heartache, and
transmuting emotional conditioning that no longer
serves you, it soothes internalized pain and heals
deprivation, so that you manifest a new pattern of
loving. If you have never received love, Rose
Quartz fills your heart. If you have loved and lost,
it comforts your grief. Rose Quartz teaches you
how to love yourself, and its assistance is vital if you
previously thought yourself unlovable. This stone
encourages the self-forgiveness and acceptance that
underlie positive self-worth.

Pink is associated with Venus, the planet of love and
desire. Amorous Venus rules passion and eroticism,
love and affection, and Rose Quartz is tender and
passionate, erotic and nurturing. This stone is one of
the most profound emotional healers on all levels,
including the karmic. Strengthening your empathy
and sensitivity, Rose Quartz gently draws off
emotional wounds and replaces them with loving
vibes. Calming and reassuring, it assists you in
manifesting necessary change.

ROSE QUARTZ AND MANIFESTATION

With its powerful emotional healing properties,
this stone is excellent during trauma or emotional
dramas. It supports you through a midlife or

other crisis that brings challenges and changes in
your life, opening you up to manifesting new
possibilities. If you feel unloved, hold Rose Quartz
and remind yourself of a time when you felt totally
positive, potent and loving. Bring that feeling into
the present to empower your manifestation.

Rose Quartz is invaluable if you are trying to
manifest something to fill a lack. It encourages you
to be emotionally honest with yourself, teaching
that you cannot fill internal black holes by external
means. The infusion of unconditional universal love
emanating from this stone helps you touch the
divine within yourself and fill yourself up from a
source that never runs dry. With its assistance, you
breathe in love and breathe it out to the world,
knowing that there is always more. This makes you
a magnet for love.

USING ROSE QUARTZ

Holding Rose Quartz assists positive affirmations.
The stone also reminds you of your intention.
When placed over your heart chakra, Rose Quartz
heals emotional wounds and infuses potent loving
energies into your heart. When placed by your bed
or in the relationship corner of your home (the
furthest right corner from your front door), it
draws love toward you. In existing relationships it
restores trust and harmony and encourages the
sharing of unconditional love.

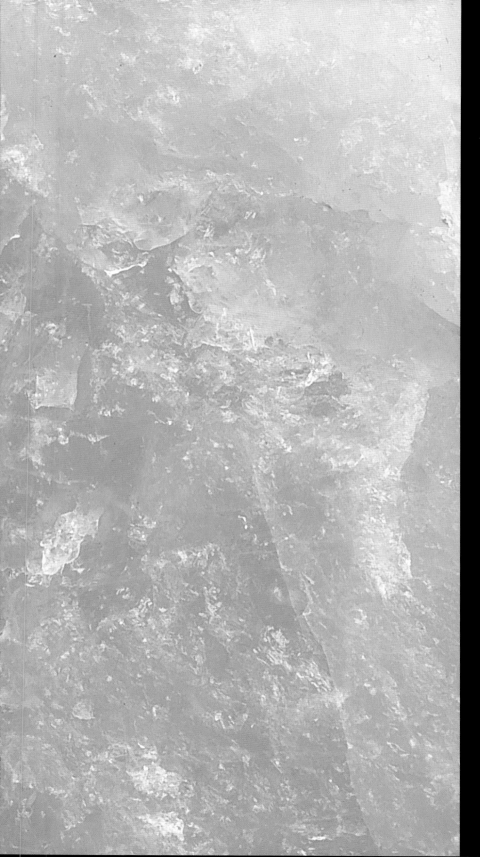

Alternative crystals

RHODOCHROSITE, TUGTUPITE, MANGANO CALCITE

Powerful heart-healers, Rhodochrosite, Tugtupite and Mangano Calcite all hold higher octaves of love that dissolve old emotional wounds. These beautiful stones radiate unconditional love and acceptance and help you find a balance in loving so that you give and receive in equal measure.

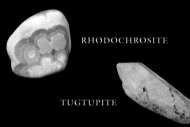

RHODOCHROSITE

TUGTUPITE

MANGANO CALCITE

GREEN AVENTURINE

Green Aventurine is a useful stone if you are of more mature years and are seeking a somewhat quieter expression of love – a steadfast one that will carry you into old age with good companionship and laughter along the way. This stone is prized for its endurance and its ability to carry abundance and good fortune into your later years.

GREEN AVENTURINE

ATTRACTING LOVE RITUAL

How can I draw love to me?

Rituals to attract love are highly potent. Whether you are looking for romance, seeking to deepen an existing relationship or ignite fresh passion, or needing to heal an old wound that is blocking the arrival of new love, crystals have the necessary power. By harnessing crystal energies through rituals, you draw more love into all areas of your life and can transform anything that may have been standing in the way. Old patterns are swept aside and new possibilities open up. When working this ritual, it is traditional to bathe and wear clean clothes – pink or red, depending on whether you seek romance or red-hot passion. The most potent time for this ritual is at the new moon. You will need five Rose Quartz crystals, some rose oil, four pink candles and a silk cloth.

1 Purify five Rose Quartz crystals and dedicate them to more love manifesting in your life. Hold the stones in your left hand and connect to their power, feeling it radiating into your manifestation chakras and throughout your whole being. If you already have a partner, ask that more love manifests between you, and that the relationship becomes the best that it has the potential to be. To add further power to the ritual, anoint yourself with rose oil. Pink candles will set the scene, and appropriate background music will assist your manifestation. When carrying out the attracting love ritual, consciously make your movements slow, moving with voluptuous intent.

2 Place four candles on a table covered with a silk cloth. Position one candle to the north, welcoming in love from that direction as you light it. Place one to the south, east and west respectively, again welcoming love from each direction. Ask that the light from these candles attracts the highest manifestation of love.

3 Hold your crystals in your hands and face your table (if the crystals are large, hold one at a time). Close your eyes and quietly attune to the crystals. Let their energy flow through your hands, up your arms and into your heart. As the energy reaches your heart, feel it open out and expand. Touch the crystals to your heart. Rose Quartz is a powerful heart-cleanser and healer, so allow your heart to be purified by the energies of the crystals

4 Say out loud, 'I am a magnet for love. I welcome love into my heart and love into my life.' Place four of the crystals around the table and pick up the final one. If you wish to manifest a lover, say out loud, 'I call on my twin flame [soulmate] to be present and to manifest fully and lovingly in my life' (or: 'I call on the love between my partner and myself to manifest to its highest potential, fully and unconditionally loving and

supporting us both'). Sit quietly for a few moments with your eyes focused on the crystals. Intensely feel what your life is like when you have the unconditional, mutually supportive love of your twin flame at your side (or when you and your partner manifest all the love that is possible between you). Send that picture out into the future, unrolling it before you so that you manifest that path. Place the crystal in the centre of the candles.

5 When you are ready to complete the ritual, get up and blow out each candle in turn, saying, 'I send light and love into the world and it returns to me tenfold.' Either leave the crystals on the table or place them around your bed.

Attracting a mentor

Mentors come in many guises, and there is a difference between a mentor and a guru. A mentor is a trusted adviser who has expertise in the area in which you wish to manifest success, be it spiritual or material. Mentors guide and direct you, supporting you in taking control of your life, and helping you to develop your own inner sense of responsibility and potency. They encourage you to grasp opportunities with both hands and go for it. Mentors empower you and are only too pleased when you achieve your full potential. They may be inner or outer figures, and may be concerned with your spiritual welfare or your financial prosperity.

A guru is an influential teacher who tells you what to do, and in return you give them absolute obedience. Gurus tend to control your life and disempower, rather than empower. They tell you how things are and what you must do to achieve success, instead of guiding you. They have their own way of doing things, which must be adhered to if you are to achieve the goals they set. Deviate and you are shunned and cut off from the group, which further disenfranchises you. If you have come under the mental control of a guru, you may need to release from this (Banded Agate placed on your third eye is really helpful here) before finding your true mentor.

Mentors may be with you for a lifetime or for a specific task. You can request that a mentor manifest to assist you in many fields. There are mentors (inner or outer) who have advanced business acumen, and others who offer innovative solutions or help you to develop necessary skills. There are mentors who pass on spiritual wisdom, and others who help you to live a fuller and more balanced life without any outward show of wealth, although with their assistance you will recognize your inner riches. A manifestation mentor assists you with all your manifesting processes. A simple visualization can connect you to exactly the right mentor for your purpose, while a manifesting crystal will help you keep the contact strong.

BLACK MOONSTONE
Your mentor crystal

A type of Labradorite, Black Moonstone is excellent for all metaphysical pursuits because it protects and opens your energy field to higher vibrations and increases your intuition. If you need a spiritual mentor or a prosperity guide, hold Black Moonstone and ask that a suitable mentor comes to you from the higher dimensions, or that one manifests in the everyday world.

UNDERSTANDING THIS CRYSTAL

Labradorite – the reflective underlying core of Black Moonstone – carries ancient spiritual wisdom at its heart. It transmutes anything negative that reaches it, so that it provides a screen for your personal energies, allowing through only what is for your highest good. It is powerfully attuned to the spiritual world, calling in guidance from the highest realms. But this stone also assists you in tuning into your own inner guidance, activating ancient wise-woman energy and bringing forward the cunning-man who knows the secret of manifestation. It draws a mentor to you.

Assisting those who are emotionally oversensitive or wide open to psychic influence, Black Moonstone filters the energetic information you pick up from other people, so that you can perceive what is useful and ignore the rest. But it also has a profound spiritual effect, helping to raise your vibrational frequency so that you attract helpful beings on the spiritual and material levels and can rise above anything that could sabotage your manifesting.

With its powerful effect on neurotransmitters, this stone is said to improve balance and memory. Moonstone is traditionally used to harmonize the female hormonal cycle and to assist during menopause. It therefore boosts wellbeing on all levels.

BLACK MOONSTONE AND MANIFESTATION

Black Moonstone is particularly useful for increasing your stamina so that you do not give up before your goal is reached. This stone gently pushes you forward toward your goal, encouraging you all the way. It helps accident-prone, dyspraxic or hyperactive children or adults become more focused, with better coordination and extended concentration, so that they can move more smoothly through life. It also assists adults who have motor difficulties, or who lack concentration, to better focus their attention and to function to the best of their ability in the everyday world.

USING BLACK MOONSTONE

This stone assists concentration, so use it for prolonged study or to enhance creativity. Place Black Moonstone around your home to attract abundance and create a calm, serene atmosphere, or to call in a mentor to help you achieve your goals. Its calming energies stabilize rocky relationships and assist during teenage angst, manifesting peace and harmony in the home.

Carry Black Moonstone with you whenever you need to call on your inner guidance to navigate challenging circumstances.

Alternative crystals

MENTOR FORMATION, KAMBABA JASPER

A Mentor Formation is a large crystal with smaller crystals around it. Meditate with one to receive inner guidance, or with Kambaba Jasper to hear the wisdom that nature offers and to find a wise mentor for your spiritual path. Resonating with the brainstem and the autonomic processes, when placed at the base of the skull Kambaba Jasper removes ingrained blockages and encourages the assimilation of new patterns.

MENTOR FORMATION

KAMBABA JASPER

SONORA SUNRISE, BANDED AGATE

Sonora Sunrise – a combination of Cuprite and Chrysocolla – also attracts a positive mentor. Overcoming difficulties with authoritarian figures and false gurus, it releases mind control. Aligning your personal will with that of your higher self, it aids in taking responsibility for your life. Place Banded Agate over your third eye to release the hold of previous gurus.

SONORA SUNRISE

BANDED AGATE

BLACK MOONSTONE VISUALIZATION

How do I meet a mentor?

This Black Moonstone visualization takes you to meet a mentor – someone who guides your life into the most productive and appropriate channels for you. Your mentor may be an inner figure or may manifest as a person in your outer life (or both). Leave the visualization as open as possible so that you make room for these figures to manifest as appropriate, but ensure that you do not manifest an authoritarian figure such as a guru. The ability of Black Moonstone to sharpen your mental focus and heighten your intuition will help you to receive signals from your mentor and recognize when opportunities present themselves.

1 Hold your cleansed and dedicated Black Moonstone in your hands and connect to its power, feeling it radiating into your manifestation chakras and throughout your whole being. Relax, close your eyes, look up to the space above and between your eyebrows and picture yourself walking in your favourite place. Setting up an easy rhythm, breathe gently, taking in all the smells and sensations that belong to that special place. If you are kinesthetic or aural rather than visual, then your mentor may make its presence known by touch, smell, words or an instinctive knowing, so open your senses to receive these impressions.

2 Ask that your mentor comes to you. Be expectant, but not insistent. Have patience. Take time to walk around, enjoying this beautiful space and the feeling of joyful anticipation that your meeting evokes. Soak in the energies of your crystal.

3 As you walk around, you may become aware that someone is coming toward you. At first it may appear as a misty figure, but will become clearer as it approaches. This is your inner mentor. Take all the time you need to get acquainted and, if necessary, spell out the kind of assistance you require. If you are to meet your mentor in the outer world, simply enjoy relaxing in this peaceful space while putting out the request that your external mentor appears soon. You may also catch a glimpse of who that mentor is.

4 When it is time to leave, thank your inner mentor for being there and arrange a call signal in case you need to get in touch. Your mentor will give you a recognition signal for future occasions, but you can also arrange that whenever you pick up your Black Moonstone your inner mentor is there.

5 Put your Black Moonstone into your pocket or handbag so that you have it with you always. You can also place it under your pillow at night to promote helpful dreams, or can activate it to attract your external mentor.

Connecting with your angels

Angels have acted as intermediaries between the Earth and the divine world over eons of time. According to esoteric lore, they were created by God at the inception of our world and adhere to cosmic law. Although sometimes looked on as a New Age phenomenon or a strictly religious concept, these winged messengers have always been active in human affairs, but have taken on various guises. The Koran was dictated to Mohammed by the Archangel Gabriel (Jibril in Islam), the selfsame messenger who brought the news of Jesus' forthcoming birth to Mary. 'Men in white' appear throughout the Old Testament, Apocryphal books and Eastern scriptures, but long beforehand these light-filled beings were depicted on ancient temples and scratched on cave walls. Angelic presence is often signalled by a wonderful perfume or the beating of wings, and an immense stillness and peace will infuse your space. But angels have been known to take on human form and to assist us without thought of recognition or reward.

These days people connect with their angels not only for guidance and as a tangible manifestation of divine love, but also from a desire for our planet as a whole to raise its vibrations so that expanded consciousness can be embodied. Angels have long been known to appear spontaneously to people at times of great trauma or need, but nowadays they are consciously invoked, and many New Agers believe that angels will soon walk on Earth alongside human beings once more. Angels are particularly amenable to kything. This ancient word describes a two-way communication with the spirit world that is very different from channelling. Kything is a conversation – your own mind is not put aside, but remains fully engaged in the process. The angelic beings suggest and offer guidance. They can be questioned or contradicted, and with infinite patience the question is addressed and the guidance refined until it is absolutely clear on both sides which is the best way forward.

No matter what your own personal belief may be, inviting angels into your life will bring you health, happiness, wise guidance and prosperity, as they enhance your manifesting powers and your spiritual life.

ANGEL'S WING CALCITE
Your angelic-connection crystal

Delicate Angel's Wing Calcite has ethereal vibrations of the finest quality, which make it the perfect receptacle for angelic energies. This beautiful crystal opens the Soul Star and Stellar Gateway chakras above your head so that you receive spiritual light and guidance from the highest levels. It opens all your metaphysical senses to perceive the angelic realm with great clarity and to communicate freely.

UNDERSTANDING THIS CRYSTAL

All Calcites have a purity of essence and spiritual cleansing properties that make them perfect for angelic work, but Angel's Wing Calcite especially embodies the power of angelic connection. Its layers hold within them the lightness of the angel wings that it resembles. Literally bringing the angelic vibration down to Earth, Angel's Wing Calcite is the perfect stone for angelic and archangelic communication.

Angel's Wing Calcite also helps you to reach the very highest of vibrations for yourself and to explore the multi-dimensions of consciousness. With this stone you become so much more aware of all that you are, on every level of your being, and harness your most potent manifesting powers.

This crystal assists you in feeling comfortable in incarnation. It integrates expanded consciousness and the lightbody with the physical body, and grounds higher-dimensional energies into the physical plane and into the Earth. At a healing level, Angel's Wing Calcite works mainly beyond the physical to harmonize the etheric, but anecdotal evidence suggests that it assists with psychosomatic dis-eases and with the underlying causes of diabetes and degenerative conditions. With its delicate strands, it stimulates new neurotransmitter pathways and harmonizes the hemispheres of the brain, so that you can use your mind more effectively as you integrate expanded awareness and higher consciousness into the lightness of your being.

ANGEL'S WING CALCITE AND MANIFESTATION

As the high vibrations of Angel's Wing Calcite stimulate the Soul Star, Stellar Gateway and other higher crown chakras to open, it brings in spiritual light to assist your manifesting. This crystal opens all psychic abilities, especially kything, and facilitates journeying through multi-dimensions. With kything, your intention is refined, your input is valued and you gain deep insight into the underlying causes of mis-manifestation – as do those who are assisting you.

USING ANGEL'S WING CALCITE

As Angel's Wing Calcite is delicate, a large piece is best used at the centre of an angel altar to focus your intention. Small pieces are also available, which can be held when meditating to connect to your angels; but avoid putting them in your pocket as they will crumble. To cleanse this stone, leave it in brown rice for a few hours and then place it in moonlight overnight.

Alternative crystals

ANGELITE, CELESTITE

Angelite is a compressed form of Celestite. Both crystals facilitate conscious connection with angelic beings, but are also stones of good fortune. Facilitating deepened attunement and heightened consciousness, they fine-tune your perception and intuition. These tranquil stones increase your compassion and your ability to love unconditionally. If you need to jump-start your manifesting, look no further, as these stones help you to trust the infinite wisdom of the divine realm.

CELESTITE

ANGELITE

AMPHIBOLE QUARTZ, AURORA QUARTZ (ANANDALITE™)

Amphibole Quartz is a magical mix of minerals that raise your vibrations to the highest level and call in angelic assistance whenever required. Iridescent, exceptionally high-vibration Aurora Quartz expands your consciousness so that you can achieve enlightenment here on Earth.

AMPHIBOLE QUARTZ

AURORA QUARTZ (ANANDALITE™)

ANGEL'S WING CALCITE ALTAR

How do I make an angelic connection?

Setting up an altar creates a sacred space and calls in your angels. It reminds you to honour your intentions and your power to manifest and maintain your angelic connection. An altar focuses your attention and helps to bring love and stillness into your heart so that your angel can speak. Position your altar in a quiet place where it will be undisturbed. You can place on it items that remind you of your manifestation goals; and fresh flowers, candles or statues will add energy to the altar. Remember to keep it fresh and clean. You will need one Angel's Wing Calcite, a silk or velvet cloth, candles, flowers and other items of your choice for your altar.

1 When you have chosen a suitable site for your altar, lay out a silk or velvet cloth in an appropriate colour for the angelic quality that you seek to manifest, or the archangel you wish to honour (see table below). Hold your crystal in your hand and connect to its power, feeling it radiating into your manifestation chakras and throughout your whole being.

2 With your left hand, place your crystal in the centre of the cloth. Position your candles, flowers and other items around it. Light the candles, if you are using them.

3 Holding your hands out to the altar, ask that the angelic beings – and any specific archangel with whom you wish to make a connection – manifest within the crystal and in your life. If you have any requests to make to your angels, set them out clearly and succinctly, raising your right hand to your forehead as you do so and leaving the left hand outstretched.

4 Spend a few moments each day focusing on your altar and giving thanks to the angelic presence in your life. You can also use the altar as a focus for longer meditation.

ARCHANGEL	COLOUR	QUALITY
Anauel	Rainbow	Prosperity and abundance
Barakiel	Rainbow	Good fortune and luck
Atrugiel	Red-black	Personal guardian
Raphael	Green	Healing
Sandalphon	Earthy	Wellbeing
Asariel	Turquoise	Intuition and insight
Azrael	Silver	Transition
Michael	Blue	Spiritual warrior, courage
Jophiel	Yellow	Cosmic wisdom
Gadiel	Smoky grey	Release from bondage
Chamuel	Pink	Divine, unconditional love
Luminel	Pale blue	Communication
Haniel	Orange	Serendipitous synchronicity
Gabriel	White	Purity of being
Uriel	Gold	Peace and rebirth
Lucifer	Black with silver	Bringing of light to dark places
Zadkiel	Violet	Transmutation
Metatron	Pure white	Ultimate harmony

Activating Higher Consciousness

Consciousness interpenetrates and shapes everything. It glues together the building blocks of matter and is the instigator of all change and transmutation on this planet and beyond. Consciousness functions in different ways. We actually operate within a very limited band of awareness: everyday consciousness. Beneath this (in terms of resonance and frequency) lie the subconscious, collective and unconscious bands of consciousness. But these are not separate from everyday consciousness – they interpenetrate and influence it at every moment. Beyond everyday awareness lie the largely unexplored and literally endless dimensions of cosmic, higher or quantum consciousness, in which everything is possible because all things already exist in potential and simply need to be activated by focused intention.

Quantum consciousness is a field that is non-local: everywhere and nowhere all at once. Higher consciousness is omniscient and omnipresent – seeing all, knowing all and creating all. It is a particle that is a wave, and a wave that is a particle. It travels backward or forward through time and demonstrates that there is no time at all. It shows that you create the event being observed. In other words, higher consciousness is a quantum field: a holographic universe with multi-dimensional awareness and mystical interconnection that has been called 'bliss consciousness', Spirit, the Source or All That Is. Higher or quantum consciousness is one of the great drivers of manifestation. It is not something set apart from ordinary consciousness, but it does need to be brought into your everyday awareness. The fastest way to do this is to meditate with high-vibration crystals, which naturally plug you into this immense source of power and insight. The term 'higher consciousness' relates to its vibratory frequency and expanded awareness, which spans multi-dimensional reality. The two are complementary and coexist as part of a whole spectrum. The 'higher' you ascend in consciousness, the more you expand your awareness, and the more permeable and malleable the connection between you and the rest of creation becomes. The more you can access this spectrum and integrate it in your daily life, the better your manifesting becomes.

AURORA QUARTZ
Your higher-consciousness crystal

Aurora Quartz, known in its trademarked form as Anandalite™, is a
naturally iridescent, exceptionally high-vibration crystal packed with
bioscalar healing waves and quantum consciousness. Integrating duality
into unity, it expands your consciousness and takes you into the
interconnectedness of all life. It harmonizes the new vibration so that
the whole of creation participates in, and benefits from, quantum uplift.

UNDERSTANDING THIS CRYSTAL

With its wonderful colour flashes, Aurora Quartz
introduces you to the limitless possibilities of
multi-dimensional being. Its exceptionally high
frequency takes you travelling through the cosmos
and beyond. Meditating with Aurora reveals the
narrow band of awareness in which you have
previously operated, and opens the gateway to
higher consciousness. Aurora crystallizes in different
forms, reflecting consciousness in all its guises.
Delicate, flower-like or 'stalactite' Drusy (or Needle)
Aurora clusters around a core and has a powerful
connection with All That Is, linking souls into unity
consciousness and cleansing the collective
consciousness. Larger crystals of Aurora hold vast
amounts of bioscalar waves and profoundly affect
the wellbeing of humanity. They are excellent for
repatterning the subconscious mind.

With its powerful bioscalar waves, Aurora activates the
body's natural healing mechanism. It reharmonizes
any dis-ease or disequilibrium created when the subtle
bodies fail to integrate higher consciousness. It also
facilitates subtle Kundalini awakening. If, however,
Kundalini has previously risen in an undirected,
disconnected fashion and has created imbalances in
the physical body, then Aurora harmonizes the
integration process and releases emotional blockages
standing in the way of spiritual awakening.

AURORA QUARTZ AND MANIFESTATION

Aurora Quartz constructs an energy grid for
bioscalar waves, higher vibrations and focused
intention to anchor into and pass through the
biomagnetic field, etheric and physical bodies of
a person or of the Earth. It de-energizes and
deconstructs any detrimental older energy structure
and enables a new pattern to be created, supporting
manifestation on every level. Each colour-flash has
specific properties. Green accesses the multi-
dimensions of consciousness. Blue amplifies the
biomagnetic field, accelerating healing. Gold repairs
and recharges healing circuits and increases the flow
of bioscalar waves. Red revitalizes and remotivates
the soul on its journey of manifestation. Brown
carries rainbow light that harmonizes and purifies
the biosphere; it brings shadows into light. This
colour carries devic and angelic energy and assists
in accessing the beings that oversee planet Earth.

USING AURORA QUARTZ

Swept from the Earth Star chakra to the crown
and back again, Anandalite purifies the whole
chakra system and aligns it to higher frequencies,
grounding the energies. This stone strips you to the
bare bones of your soul, and patiently rebuilds your
energy patterns so that you accommodate a massive
consciousness shift and manifest enlightenment.

Alternative crystals

ALL HIGH-VIBRATION
QUARTZES, SUCH AS
AZEZTULITE, RAINBOW
MAYANITE, TRIGONIC,
SATYAMANI, SATYALOKA
QUARTZ™, PETALITE,
PHENACITE

Many new high-vibration stones
are coming onto the market. All
of them effortlessly connect you
to higher consciousness, each
seemingly superseding the
dimension to which previous stones
ascended. Which one you choose
depends on your starting point.
Experienced crystal workers choose
the latest stones, such as Azeztulite,
Rainbow Mayanite and Trigonic,
or new finds to accelerate their
soul-journey, while beginners might
more sensibly start with tried-and-
tested Satyamani, Satyaloka, Petalite
or Phenacite to open the way.

AZEZTULITE

RAINBOW
MAYANITE

TRIGONIC

SATYAMANI

SATYALOKA
QUARTZ™

PHENACITE

PETALITE

AURORA QUARTZ MEDITATION

How do I connect to higher consciousness?

Sitting quietly, holding a high-vibration crystal, instantly transports you to the highest possible dimensions of consciousness. The more you raise your own vibrational frequency, the higher dimension you will reach. You ascend a ladder by choosing a succession of stones that progressively take you higher and higher. Or you could try one of the new, exceptionally high-vibration stones that shoot you straight to the peak of bliss consciousness (like an express-train). Much depends on your own individual response to a specific crystal. But whichever stones or method you choose, remember to ground the new vibration into your body, so that your higher consciousness can manifest here on Earth.

1 Hold your Aurora Quartz in your hand and connect to its power, feeling it radiating into your manifestation chakras and throughout your whole being. Allow the powerful bioscalar waves in the crystal to pulsate throughout your physical and subtle bodies. Feel how it realigns subtle meridians (channels), cells and cellular transmitters, reconfiguring your physical and psychic immune system and reordering your electrical circuits and central nervous system, to accommodate the flow of quantum consciousness. Take as long as necessary for this essential process.

2 When you feel ready, touch your Aurora Quartz to your Dantien (just below your navel), then to the soma chakra (midway along your hairline), and then as far as you can reach over your head.

3 Let the crystal lie in your hands in your lap. Feel the luminescent, subtle Kundalini force of the crystal being drawn up through the central channel of your body, activating all the chakras

from the base into the head and connecting to the very highest. This ignites spiritual awakening and quantum consciousness. Dissolving the barriers between the different levels of creation, it takes you into the infinite possibilities of the universal mind.

4 Allow yourself to ride the waves of that higher consciousness. Do not try to control it, merely have the intention to explore and experience it. Ask the crystal to take you through the multi-dimensions of consciousness and into the ones that are most appropriate for you at this time. You may not be able to explain quantum physics coherently when you emerge, but you will have intimately experienced it and the beautiful, holographic universe that is multi-dimensional consciousness and mystical interconnectedness. Remind yourself that you can enter this state at any time simply by raising your vibrational frequency – your Aurora Quartz is always ready to assist, but your mind soon learns how to do it without crystalline assistance.

5 When the meditation is complete, place the Aurora Quartz at your feet and consciously direct the higher energies to ground themselves into the Earth. Thank your crystal for its work. Stand up and feel your feet making a powerful connection with the planet. If you feel light-headed, hold Hematite or Smoky Quartz to ground you.

6 Put your Aurora Quartz in a place where it can continue to radiate its powerful healing and integration energies into your environment and into the Earth.

Reconnecting to perfection

At the highest level of soul you are a perfect being. Before time began, you arose from pure consciousness and a pool of spiritual essence that held no imperfections. Some people call this the divine, others God or Spirit, or All That Is. It doesn't matter what you name it – it simply is. Way back, your soul decided to set out on a journey of exploration, leaving this state of perfection behind. However, it carried with it an energetic imprint, a hologram of the divine, a subtle etheric grid or blueprint that, at its heart, holds the seed of perfection that travels with you over eons of time and the multi-dimensions of being.

Why did it leave, you may ask? The consciousness that is your soul wanted to know itself. To do this, it had to descend through many layers and levels of experience into denser and lower vibrations until, eventually, it manifested in the physical world. It formed groups and fragmented again, gave itself away, gathered pieces that did not belong to its pure self, became entangled and hooked into other soul-grids. Along the way the perfect grid gathered karmic encrustations and soul-wounds from past lives – ancestral crud that adhered through the DNA of the family line – and imprints of the many experiences it had. It forgot that it was pure consciousness and part of the original pool of spiritual essence that was perfection. It took on ego and self-centredness, emotional and mental imprints, relationships with other people, physical challenges and enormous suffering. It forgot its divine origins and believed that something else was God. All of this left an imprint on the etheric grid. From this grid were manifested the many bodies in which the soul ultimately had its human experiences. The blockages, wounds and encrustations that it carried showed up as physical or psychological dis-eases.

But the innate integrity and potential of the etheric grid remained – together with its connection to all other grids, whatever form they may have taken on. They were one. At its heart it was pure perfection – a perfection that can be regained, and which facilitates manifesting at the highest level in all spheres of life.

BRANDENBERG
Your perfection crystal

Brandenberg has exceedingly high vibrations, connecting to the immensity of your being and All That Is. This is a powerful stone for spiritual alchemy and is perfect for deep soul-healing. It helps you retain awareness of traversing other dimensions and the insights that you find there. Multi-functional, each stone carries the resonance of Clear, Smoky and Amethyst vibrations no matter what its colour.

UNDERSTANDING THIS CRYSTAL

Brandenbergs are unique. Found in Namibia, where powerful synchoic Earth-energy lines cross, they are imbued with extremely potent healing energy. The inclusions and phantoms within the stone act like a ladder to higher dimensions. Brandenberg attunes you to your core spiritual identity, activating higher consciousness and connection with the multi-dimensions of the spiritual world. It restores to its perfect energetic state the etheric blueprint from which your physical body was formed, taking it to the highest vibration of All That Is: perfection. It restores balance to the mental, psychological, emotional and physical bodies and to the ancestral and karmic blueprints.

BRANDENBERG AND MANIFESTATION

Brandenberg assists travel to the between-lives state, to ascertain your soul-plan for your current lifetime. It returns you to your original plan if you have deviated, and releases outgrown soul-imperatives. Healing the imprints and effects of trauma in previous lives (no matter in what dimension those lives were lived), it restores your power to manifest wisely. Brandenberg also removes blockages to spiritual sight and accesses guidance from the purest source. This protective stone assists during soul-retrieval or child-parts retrieval (reintegrating parts of the soul that split off in childhood) and facilitates purification and integration of those parts into your present self.

USING BRANDENBERG

A Brandenberg clears the higher heart chakra and opens the throat, so that spiritual truth is spoken with unconditional love and compassion. A master healer, it restores vitality by taking you into the most perfect energetic state possible and activating the divine hologram within your soul.

Although individual Brandenbergs carry the vibration of Smoky, Amethyst and Clear, each colour assists differently. Smoky Brandenberg is the finest tool for removing implants, attachments, spirit possession or mental influence; it assists conscious transition. If you took on a dis-ease – physical or psychosomatic – or traumatic circumstances for karma or soul-growth, then Smoky Brandenberg helps you face the remainder of your current life with equanimity and joy, knowing that your situation is exactly right for your evolution. Amethyst Brandenberg heals past-life heartbreak or soul-contracts, manifesting a partner who totally supports who you are, while Clear Brandenberg reconnects you to the purity of your being.

Alternative crystals

AURORA QUARTZ (ANANDALITE™), SATYALOKA QUARTZ™, NIRVANA QUARTZ

Naturally iridescent Aurora Quartz has exceptionally high vibrations that integrate duality into unity, taking you into the interconnectedness of all life and harmonizing the new vibration to create a quantum uplift. Satyaloka Quartz has had its vibration raised by spiritual light; it creates profound union with the divine and opens the highest levels of mystical consciousness. Nirvana Quartz – a naturally high-vibration Quartz from the Himalayas – facilitates a shift into the enlightenment of inner bliss. Standing at the interface of consciousness and matter, mind and body, spirit and soul, past and future, human and divine, Nirvana Quartz is crystallized perfection.

AURORA QUARTZ (ANANDALITE™)

SATYALOKA QUARTZ™

NIRVANA QUARTZ

PHANTOM QUARTZ

If the new high-vibration Quartzes are not available to you, then Phantom Quartz can be ascended like a ladder to cleanse old patterns.

PHANTOM QUARTZ

THE JOURNEY TO PERFECTION

How can I reconnect to perfection?

The phantoms, layers and inclusions within Brandenberg act as a ladder to higher dimensions. This journey takes you through subtle energies to reach the perfect energy pattern at the core of the universe and of your being. It strips away everything that was imprinted on the perfect blueprint that your soul started with on its journey into incarnation. It removes karmic encrustations, soul-wounds, blockages, beliefs and imperfections, no matter where they arose from. It then reveals and re-imprints the perfect energy pattern that holds all possibilities and potential for you and your future –and that of generations to come.

1 Hold your Brandenberg in your hand and connect to its power, feeling it radiating into your manifestation chakras and throughout your whole being. Settle yourself quietly and breathe gently, withdrawing your attention from the outside world and into the crystal. Keeping your eyes half-open, let them go out of focus, and gaze at the phantoms and inclusions within your Brandenberg.

2 Feel the crystal taking you to the foot of the ladder to higher dimensions. The first rung takes you through your own aura, helping you to purify blockages and expand your awareness. It passes through the physical level, so that old blockages, encrustations and wound imprints are removed. It then moves through the emotional level, so that ingrained toxic emotions fall away and the emotional aura is purified. It passes through the mental level, so that toxic beliefs and mental imprints are let go. It clears entities, hooks and attachments that you have gathered over your long soul-journey. Your aura may feel more than a little holey with so much released, but crystal light floods in to keep the spaces open for new patterning when appropriate.

3 The second rung takes you through your ancestral heritage, cleansing and healing the ancestral line as you go. It sends healing back down through all the branches of the family tree, and forward into future generations.

4 The third rung takes you up to meet your soul, and the higher self that sees so much further than you are able to access, when cloaked with the energies of the Earth plane. It helps you to cleanse and release your karmic past.

5 The fourth rung takes you to the highest dimension possible and cleanses your spiritual being, releasing soul-wounds and imperatives that no longer serve you. It releases hooks and entanglements, soul-contracts and attachments that arose from them. Spend some time here to garner and recollect your spiritual wisdom and your true purpose.

6 The Brandenberg then takes you to where your pure spiritual essence – the perfect blueprint of all that you are, and all that you can be – awaits you. Step into this blueprint and absorb the new patterns and potentials that it offers. Feel it reconnecting to the divine hologram, adjusting and harmonizing through all the levels of your being, until it settles into the physical, so that you manifest optimum wellbeing and your soul's true purpose.

7 When you are ready to return, bring your consciousness back down the ladder and disconnect your eyes from the stone. Your focus becomes sharper, until you touch the Earth plane once more. Settle your awareness comfortably back into your physical body. Breathe a little deeper. Move your fingers and toes, stretch and slowly stand up, ensuring that your feet make contact with the Earth. If you feel light-headed, place a Smoky Quartz between your feet and hold some Hematite in your hands.

Opening the soul-doorway

Most of the universe (as with our bodies) is 'empty space' filled with dynamic energy, and we can look on the soul as a vehicle for that cosmic energy, but the energy permeates through the soul and the physical body together; it is not separate. Being connected to your soul opens a conduit to higher consciousness and manifestation powers of the highest order.

It is clear from past-life regressions, near-death and out-of-body experiences, spontaneous recall and communications beyond death that the most singular characteristic of a soul is its aliveness. It is conscious and aware, capable of movement and choice, and has a cohesive identity. It is also clear that the soul inhabits many different dimensions and timeframes, *all at the same time*, because it is holographic. It reflects and experiences through each and every part of itself, even when seemingly fragmented. Energetic rather than physical, a soul-hologram can communicate with, and receive experiences from, its many forms within the one. If the soul chooses to shine the light of awareness through a different part of the holographic pattern, it reflects a different attitude of mind and gives the soul a whole new perspective on an old issue, or opens up new areas to be explored.

We have a 'small self' soul-part down here in incarnation at the densest vibration of being: the physical. But we also have a 'higher self' soul-part that is not fully incarnated and which has access to other realms of being. It is much wiser than 'me-down-here'. This higher self knows what soul-contracts have been made, the full extent of the soul-plan for the present incarnation and where it fits into the soul's overall evolutionary plan, as well as the soul's history. It keeps track of incarnatory experiences and guides the soul toward understanding and fulfilment. The higher self is in contact with the Akashic Record, which holds the imprint of all that has been and will be. So being more in touch with your soul makes you more able to manifest who you really are.

YOUR SOUL CRYSTAL
Trigonic Quartz

Characterized by upside-down triangles cascading down one or more of its faces, the Trigonic soul-symbol is appearing on many high-vibration stones and carries cosmic DNA codes and pure soul-essence. Trigonic Quartz acts as a soul-midwife and opens the door to your soul in all its manifestations. The stone takes you to the core of who you are and who you are meant to be.

UNDERSTANDING THIS CRYSTAL

Trigonic Quartz is a profound tool for personal and planetary evolution. Its power lies in its deep connection to the soul and unity consciousness. Trigonics facilitate moving between different levels of reality with grace and ease. They carry holographic soul DNA and act as a united whole. Trigonic Quartz helps you transcend the boundaries of everyday reality. Everyone who works with it has a unique personal experience. Trigonics have solidified and made themselves known in order to help the transition to expanded awareness, and they need compatible, harmonious human consciousness to facilitate their work. Working with Trigonics opens subtle high-dimensional chakras to an influx of spiritual reality and propels you into expanded awareness. Once you experience quantum consciousness, your vibratory rate is permanently changed to a higher frequency.

The triangular markings on the crystal faces look chiselled, but this is a natural formation that can appear at any time. The energy-being that is the Trigonic oversoul is moving from a plasmic state to a crystalline one. It is undergoing profound metamorphosis itself and assists you to make a similar transmutation. The effect is fast, furious – and highly focused.

TRIGONIC QUARTZ AND MANIFESTATION

Creating a calm core around which everything rushes and flows, Trigonic Quartz facilitates you being 'here' and 'there' at the same time and knowing that all is one. Making you stay with what is in any given moment, Trigonic reconnects you to your highest purpose rather than what your ego might desire. When working with this crystal it is essential to have released blockages and toxicity from the physical and subtle bodies, as well as the higher-dimensional chakras, because otherwise unresolved issues will surface and may induce a dramatic catharsis. After this, you are connected to your soul at the highest level. When manifesting from this level, you work for the highest good of all. In anchoring higher consciousness to Earth, you raise the evolutionary consciousness of the planet.

USING TRIGONIC QUARTZ

Holding this stone takes you instantly into quantum consciousness to gain an objective overview on your soul's journey. Meditating with Trigonic triggers a simultaneous beta-theta brainwave state that enables deep healing and restructuring of the body, beliefs and realities to occur. Trigonic Quartz manifests peace in any conflict situation.

Alternative crystals

CRYSTAL CAP AMETHYST (SNOW CAP)

Crystal Cap Amethyst acts like a ladder to ascended awareness and brings you back to your body, to integrate quantum consciousness when the experience is complete. This crystal harmonizes the brain, encouraging integration of the various parts, and activates neurotransmitters and new neural pathways so that you manifest anew.

CRYSTAL CAP AMETHYST

MYSTIC MERLINITE, PHENACITE

Mystic Merlinite rapidly expands consciousness. It facilitates exploring the hidden parts of your psyche, to better understand situations that had a profound effect on your manifesting. Phenacite is useful if you are setting out on the journey to unite your personal awareness with higher consciousness; it heals the soul and purifies the subtle and physical bodies to manifest higher consciousness on Earth.

MYSTIC MERLINITE

PHENACITE

TRIGONIC MEDITATION
How do I reconnect to my soul and its purpose?

As your soul sees so much further than the part of you that is incarnated in the dense vibrations of the Earth, a strong soul-connection from which to manifest makes good sense. Stepping into this higher-vibration self enables you to look at the plans you made before coming into incarnation: your soul-mission. Some people plan their new incarnation extremely carefully, while others pop back without much thought. Both are drawn back by unfinished business – the difference being in how (or whether) they plan to deal with it. Those who plan usually have an intention to develop spiritually. However, just as our down-here-self can have unconscious desires and imperatives born out of previous conditioning that is directing our behaviour, so can the soul. If you had a soul-purpose in the past and it was not fulfilled, then it could still be operating unconsciously and might have subtly perverted your present intent. This meditation helps you to identify and reframe any such outdated purpose.

1 Hold your stone in your hand and connect to its power, feeling it radiating into your manifestation chakras and throughout your whole being.

2 Gaze at the triangles on your stone – each one showing you a facet of yourself and acting as a gateway to the holograph of your soul. Allow these facets to communicate energetically with you, telling you the story of your soul's journey, with its highs and lows, credits and deficits, wisdom and awareness. Feel the immense breadth of your soul.

3 If there are any parts of your soul that have fragmented or remain caught elsewhere in time, ask that these parts return to you via the crystal, so that the energy is purified and returned to its highest vibration. Welcome the parts home.

4 Ask that your soul makes clear to you the purpose of your present-life incarnation, the soul-mission you are on and how you may best carry this out. Ask what soul-contracts you have made with other people that are to be fulfilled in this present lifetime.

5 Ask your soul to indicate any negative, past-its-sell-by-date soul-imperative, soul-contract or outdated purpose that may be interfering with carrying out your soul-mission. When you find it, explain to the soul-part that is carrying that outdated purpose or contract that it no longer applies, that you have moved on in your evolution and it is time to dissolve it and let it go.

6 Your crystal draws your attention to a doorway outlined in the brightest of celestial light, beyond which sparkling triangles dance and sing. Let the energies of the crystal pass you through this gateway to the very highest energetic frequency of your soul. Rest in this energy and absorb it.

7 When it is time to return, bring that contact with your soul back with you, anchoring it into your heart. Place the crystal where you will see it often, to remind you to manifest from your soul.

8 Stand up, feel the contact that your feet make with the floor and then take your soul out into the world.

Bringing magic into your life

This whole book has been about creating a magical life for yourself – one with room for serendipity and synchronicity, passion and dreaming, creativity and joyful manifestation, soul and soul-fullness. Now it is time to draw it all together. By this stage you'll have cleared out those background thoughts, transformed your negative emotions into positive ones, attuned to quantum consciousness and the incredible breadth of your soul, gained the gift of inner happiness and contentment, and learned how to be a bliss-magnet. You'll have recognized that prosperity and abundance are much more than material wealth, and will have transformed any toxic programmes that you were broadcasting and will now be putting out signals to the universe that attract back only the highest and the best.

So what's left? Well, it's time to let a world of wonder and magic unfold. To create a life full of magic moments. Life is pretty magical, when you stop and think about it. After all, you are standing on a planet that is spinning rapidly in space at hundreds of miles an hour and you aren't falling off. Nor do you even realize that you are spinning – magic in itself! You are composed of millions of atoms, most of which comprise empty space, and yet you have a material form. But your awareness can leave that form behind and go travelling. You have an imagination that can create anything or any place you desire – and you have the power to bring that into manifested being.

The magical keys:
- Follow your passion.
  - Use the power of your imagination.
    - Invest in your heart's desires.
      - Believe in yourself.
        - Be thankful, feel blessed.

Create your own magical dream!

MERLINITE
Your magical crystal

A combination of Quartz and Psilomelane, Merlinite brings magic into your life. This holographic stone holds the combined wisdom of wonder-workers, shamans, alchemists, wizards, magician-priests and practitioners of magic throughout all ages. Blending spiritual and earthly vibrations, uniting above and below in a magical correspondence that passes the power of the gods into the Earth, it facilitates access to the spiritual dimensions and to the magical, shamanic realms.

UNDERSTANDING THIS CRYSTAL

Merlinite was named after the legendary King Arthur's magician-mentor. A reflective stone, this dendritic Agate is perfect for magical working because its delicately branching tendrils and flowing layers create pathways that subtly penetrate the veils between the visible and invisible worlds. It helps you to feel secure and protected whilst traversing the unknown. This stone opens your intuitive channels and harmonizes the neural pathways in the brain to make it more receptive to alchemical, synergistic magic. It attracts mentors and allies from other worlds when you first learn the art of magic or shamanism. The darker portions of Merlinite can lead you into the underworld of your own self, facilitating shamanic journeying for soul-retrieval and core soul-healing. It helps you to accept and integrate your shadow qualities, in which lie your greatest gifts.

A stone that attracts serendipitous synchronicity and shamanistic transmutation, Merlinite aligns you with the universal flow and facilitates the manifestation of cosmic forces in the material world. Having a powerful connection with the elements, it was traditionally used for weather magic and fertility.

MERLINITE AND MANIFESTATION

Merlinite helps you to understand your soul's destiny. It also helps you to accept that what you think you need may not be what is required for your highest growth and good. A stone of synthesis and integration, it connects your intellect with your intuition, the subconscious with the conscious mind, darkness with light, and unites masculine and feminine in an alchemical marriage of unlimited creation.

Merlinite assists in reading the Akashic Record of your soul, inducing travel into the interlife or past or future lives, so that you reframe and heal incidents that would otherwise lead to ineffective manifestation. Souls play out the destinies planned in the space between lives, although this plan may be sabotaged by accrued karma and by outdated soul-plans from other lives. When accessing the Akashic Record, you see what you have been and what you might be – your potential futures, depending on the choices you make now.

USING MERLINITE

When faced with choices, place Merlinite over your third eye to see the potential consequences and to manifest a desirable outcome. By harnessing its power, you can learn your soul-purpose.

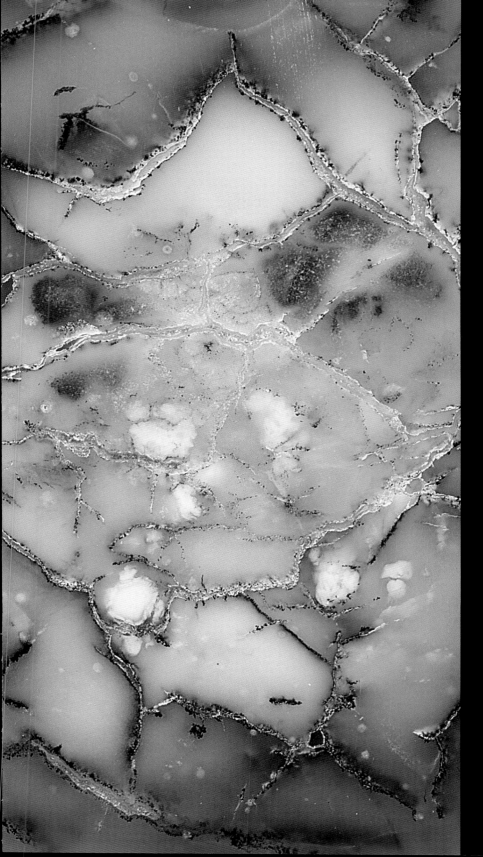

Alternative crystals

STAUROLITE, STIBNITE

Staurolite supports magical rituals and enhances communication between the worlds. Stibnite is the shaman's stone: facilitating shapeshifting, it creates a powerful shield around the body while it is journeying. When used as a wand, it separates the pure from the dross and reveals the gold in your core.

STAUROLITE

STIBNITE

BRONZITE, MOHAWKITE

Bronzite creates a clear space for magical working. This stone helps you to enter a state of 'non-being', bringing you to a place of total serenity. If you have become stuck in a negative pattern, Bronzite releases you into the universal flow. Mohawkite combines the stability and perceptiveness of metal with the transmutational possibilities of cobalt. Excellent for working simultaneously at a higher dimension and within the Earth's frequency, it grounds vibrational change and harnesses subtle-energy fields to create magic.

BRONZITE

MOHAWKITE

MERLINITE MAGICAL MANIFESTATION

How can I bring magic into my life?

Magical lore teaches that whatever the magic of your mind imagines is manifested in the material world. Taking time out to create magical moments imbues your life with potent magic, and grounds your manifestation wishes into everyday life. Sending out your desires, and then calling down and anchoring the universal creative flow, manifests a never-ending cycle of continuous manifestation. Giving away something that you value is the first step to manifesting abundance. The time-honoured receptacle and creator of magic is the cauldron, which represents the womb of creation; and the universal symbol for manifestation is the pentangle, a fluidly flowing sigil – a magical shape that creates, gathers in and generates out again. So you will need a 'cauldron' (you can use a large, flat-bottomed glass or metal bowl, or a crystal bowl if you have one) and a round piece of card that fits inside it, plus a pen, five Merlinite crystals and five candles.

1 Before commencing this ritual, freely give away something that you treasure. Give it to the first person that you meet or hear about whose life would be enriched by the gift. If possible, give it anonymously.

2 On a round piece of card that fits inside your 'cauldron', draw a pentangle without pausing. In the centre of the pentangle draw or place a picture of the magical, all-seeing eye (the eye that literally sees everything, going way beyond consensual reality into all possibilities and dimensions). Place your diagram in the bottom of your cauldron.

3 Into your cauldron breathe compassion and love for all. Fill it with thoughts of gratitude and blessing.

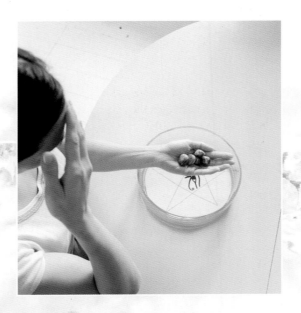

4 Hold your cleansed stones in your left hand and connect to their power, feeling it radiating into your manifestation chakras and throughout your whole being. Hold your left hand with the stones over the cauldron, then place your right hand to your third eye and call in the highest cosmic power, to open the pentangle and link to the all-seeing eye in the centre. Invite your own inner, all-seeing eye to open.

5 With your right hand, place a stone at the top of the pentangle, calling down the magic of the universe as you do so. Place another stone at the bottom right of the pentangle and the next one at the middle left. Move across to the middle right and place a fourth stone. Place the last stone at the bottom left, then take your hand back up to the first stone.

6 Around the cauldron, place candles at the five points of the pentangle and light each one, calling in the highest magical forces and the light of the universe as you do so. Invite magical moments to enter your life. Radiate them out all around you to light your path and brighten the lives of others.

7 Gaze at the glowing pentangle until you can shut your eyes and still see it clearly. During the days and weeks that follow, take a moment or two to stop what you are doing, close your eyes, create that glowing pentangle again and invite high magic to manifest in your life.

GLOSSARY

AKASHIC RECORD: a cosmic record that exists beyond time and space, containing information on all that has occurred and all that will occur

ALL THAT IS: Spirit, the Source, the divine: the sum total of everything that is

ANCESTRAL LINE: the means by which family patterns and beliefs are passed from previous generations

AURA: the subtle-energy body around the physical body

BETWEEN-LIVES STATE: the vibratory state in which the soul resides between incarnations

BIOMAGNETIC ENERGY: the subtle, organized electromagnetic energy that surrounds the human body as well as all living things (including crystals)

BIOMAGNETIC SHEATH: the subtle-energy body around the physical body, comprising physical, emotional, mental and spiritual layers

BIOSCALAR ENERGY/WAVES: a standing energy field created when two electromagnetic fields counteract each other, which directly influences tissue at the microscopic level, bringing about healing balance. Research has shown that bioscalar waves increase the circulation, enhance the immune and endocrine systems, improve the coherence of the biomagnetic field and support healing at all levels.

CELLULAR MEMORY: the memory of past lives or ancestral attitudes, trauma and patterns carried by the cells, which has become deeply ingrained as ongoing negative programmes that create dis-ease or are replayed in the present in slightly different forms

CENTRAL CHANNEL: an energetic tube running up the centre of the body (close to the spine) linking the chakras and higher consciousness; it forms the pathway for Kundalini (see below)

CHAKRA: an energy linkage point between the physical and subtle bodies. Malfunction leads to physical, emotional, mental or spiritual dis-ease or disturbance.

CORE BELIEFS: ancient, deeply held, often unconscious beliefs that have been passed down through the ancestral line or the soul's lineage and which powerfully affect behaviour in the present. Core beliefs may be at odds with what the conscious mind believes it wants.

DANTIEN: a small, spirally rotating, power-generating sphere that sits on top of the sacral chakra. If it is empty or depleted, creative energy cannot function fully, resulting in unbalance. Draining occurs through sexual acts that are not fully loving and supportive, through overwork and people pulling on your energy.

DE-ENERGIZE: take the emotional charge out of a negative emotion or mental construct to open room for a positive feeling or belief to express itself

DETOXIFIER: a substance that draws toxins out of the body

DIS-EASE: the state that results from physical imbalances, blocked feelings, suppressed emotions and negative thinking, which (if not reversed) leads to illness

EARTH STAR CHAKRA: located about 30 cm (12 in) beneath the feet, this is your linkage point to the nurturing energy of Mother Earth. It holds you in physical incarnation and grounds you on the planet.

ETHERIC BLUEPRINT: the subtle-energetic programme from which the subtle and physical bodies are constructed. It carries imprints of past-life dis-ease, injuries and beliefs, which present life conditions may reflect.

ETHERIC BODY: the subtle biomagnetic sheath surrounding the physical body

EXPANDED AWARENESS: an expanded spectrum of consciousness that encompasses the grounded, lower frequencies of Earth and the higher frequencies of multi-dimensions. Being in a state of expanded awareness facilitates accessing every level of reality and all timeframes simultaneously.

FACETED: relating to the flat, polished side of a cut gemstone or natural crystal

GENERATOR: either a Quartz cluster with points radiating out in all directions or a large point with six equal-sided faces meeting in a point in the middle. It creates energy and radiates it out to the world around you.

GRID: the placing of crystals in a specific pattern

GROUNDING: creating a strong connection between your soul, your physical body and the Earth

HIGHER CONSCIOUSNESS: an expanded spectrum of consciousness that encompasses the grounded, lower frequencies of Earth and the higher frequencies of multi-dimensions

INCLUSIONS: see Phantoms

KARMA: the principle that 'what goes around comes around' – or the sum total of all that has gone before. Karma is a dynamic, self-creating round that governs present life, but also encompasses actions from your past experience and your future potential.

KINESTHESIA: body-sensing, or having the ability to feel things rather than see them

KUNDALINI POWER: an inner, subtle, creative, spiritual and sexual energy that resides at the base of the spine and, when awakened, rises to the crown chakra. Kundalini energy is also found in the Earth.

KYTHING: two-way communication with the spirit world

LAW OF ATTRACTION: the principle that 'like attracts like'

LAYOUT: the placing of crystals in a specific pattern

MENTAL INFLUENCES: the effect of other people's thoughts and strong opinions on your mind

NEGATIVE EMOTIONAL PROGRAMMING: 'oughts' and 'shoulds' and emotions such as guilt, which have been instilled – often in childhood or other lives – and remain in the subconscious mind, influencing your present behaviour and sabotaging the ability to manifest, until they are released

PHANTOMS AND INCLUSIONS: the pyramid shapes, small crystals or mineral fragments and bubbles within a crystal point

PSYCHOSOMATIC: relating to an illness caused by toxic emotions, such as jealousy, bitterness and resentment, or ingrained belief patterns and expectations, which becomes a physical dis-ease. For instance, if someone is hard-hearted, this may manifest as hardening of the arteries.

QI: the universal life force

REFRAMING: seeing a past event in a different, more positive light so that the dis-ease it is creating is healed

SOUL-PLAN: the soul's intention and learning plan for the present life, which may have been carefully reviewed in the between-lives state or may be a knee-jerk reaction to karmic causes

STELLAR GATEWAY CHAKRA: located about as high as you can reach above your head, this chakra is a cosmic portal to other dimensions and to communication with enlightened beings

SUBTLE ENERGY: a subtle biomagnetic energy capsule that surrounds and interpenetrates the physical body and works in harmony with the physical and psychic bodies to mediate energy flow

THIRD EYE: the source of insight, located in the centre of the forehead, between and slightly above the eyebrows

THOUGHT FORMS: forms created by strong positive or negative thoughts, which exist on the etheric or spiritual level and affect someone's mental functioning

TRANSMUTATION: a change for the better in energy, or an inbuilt pattern so that your potential can emerge

TUMBLED CRYSTALS: crystals that have been polished and had their rough edges removed

TWIN FLAME: this is what most people call a soulmate, although a twin flame does not have karma, soul-lessons or soul-promises, or unfinished business attached

VISUALIZATION: the art of seeing things in your mind's eye

INDEX

FURTHER READING

Mike Eastwood, *The Crystal Oversoul Cards* (Forres, 2011)
Judy Hall, *The Book of Why: Understanding your soul's journey* (Bournemouth, 2010)
Judy Hall, *The Crystal Bible*, vols 1 and 2 (London, 2009)
Judy Hall, *The Crystal Experience* (London, 2010)
Judy Hall, *Crystal Prescriptions* (Ropley, 2005)
Judy Hall, *Crystal Prosperity* (Lewes, 2010)
Judy Hall, *Good Vibrations* (Bournemouth, 2009)

ACKNOWLEDGEMENTS

AUTHOR ACKNOWLEDGEMENTS

My thanks, as always, to the many crystal suppliers who have unstintingly shared their knowledge and new finds with me. I am grateful to Robert Simmonds for permission to use the names of stones that he has trademarked (indicated by ™ in the text) and to other crystal workers too numerous to mention. My workshops participants, friends and clients have done sterling work in testing out the layouts and visualizations in this book, and I thank them. My mentor Christine Hartley set me on the path to successful manifesting by teaching me the necessity of focusing my thoughts and controlling my emotions; and others have added to that knowledge over the years – I thank you all. I also owe a debt of gratitude to David Eastoe of Petaltone, without whose cleansing essences I could not work with crystals. Crystals attuned by Judy Hall are available from www.angeladditions.co.uk.

PUBLISHER ACKNOWLEDGEMENTS

Thank you to Mysteries (www.mysteries.co.uk), Tina May (www. crystalmaster.co.uk) and The London Astrology Shop (www.astrology.co.uk) for lending us some of their crystals for photography.

PICTURE ACKNOWLEDGEMENTS

All photography © Octopus Publishing Group/Lyanne Wylde: except for page 105
Harry Taylor/Getty Images

Commissioning Editor: Liz Dean
Managing Editor: Clare Churly
Deputy Art Director: Yasia Williams-Leedham
Design: www.gradedesign.com
Special photography: Lyanne Wylde
Models: Elle Benton and Jacqueline Freeman
Make-up Artist: Victoria Barnes
Picture Library Manager: Jennifer Veall
Production Controller: Allison Gonsalves